How *One Flesh* touched my life!

I read this book, first, because of its author, my dear friend and fellow minister who may be the most able teacher of the Word I've ever heard, and second, because of the title, *One Flesh*.

As I read and paused to meditate on Bob's wise words, deep thinking and honest reciting of his own failures in his marriage to lovely Loretta, I said, "This book is for me, and for Evelyn, although we've had a near perfect marriage for fifty-four glad years."

Then I began to wish I had known some of Bob's revelations on the Word regarding man and wife living together as one flesh because I saw how much better Evelyn's and my marriage could have been, how much better examples to our children we could have been and how much greater a legacy we could have left behind.

This is absolutely the best book on love, sexual romance, joy and compatibility in marriage I've ever read. I pray thousands upon thousands — single, married, divorced or remarried — will get their own copy of *One Flesh*. I plan to read my copy at least once a year. I still have so much to learn!

Thank You, Lord, for Bob and Loretta Yandian and for this gutsy, frank and scripturally sound book, *One Flesh*.

Oral Roberts
Oral Roberts University
Tulsa, Oklahoma

Guaranteed to make you think!

Here is a book on the ever-popular subject of love and marriage that might draw a few gasps from Christian readers.

Bob Yandian never departs from his biblical base as he explores the most intimate problems of the conjugal relationship, but some may not be prepared for the bold incisiveness of his interpretations of particular scriptures

1

relating to sex and marriage! This book is guaranteed to make you think.

D. James Kennedy, Ph.D.
Coral Ridge Presbyterian Church
Fort Lauderdale, Florida

Single or married, this book must be read!

As an author, this is the book I wish I had written! Bob Yandian has given a teacher's treatise on the marriage relationship as only he can. He presents biblical truth in practical reality, depicting marriage as the honorable covenant God made it to be.

One Flesh needs to be a textbook for every Christian who is married, but single or married, you must read this book!

Dr. Edwin Louis Cole
Men's Christian Network
Dallas, Texas

The teachings in this book saved my marriage.

Many books have been written about marriage, from many points of view, but I do not know of one that has impacted me more drastically than this. What you are about to read is insight from God's point of view. Without any question, it saved my marriage.

My wife, Lynne, and I were serving the Lord the best we knew how, but we had many problems associated with our past. Our marriage was a disaster, and we were on the brink of divorce. Reluctantly, we sought Pastor Bob's help. We were both wounded and felt there was no hope. We just wanted the pain to end. He counseled us and gave us his tape series "One Flesh." The richness of the Word of God in that teaching set us free. God restored our marriage, and today we are stronger than ever.

When I received the manuscript of this book, I couldn't hold back the tears as I remembered how God used Pastor Bob and this powerful teaching in our lives. There are

2

many who need to read it. I don't know of any marriage that couldn't benefit from God's wisdom represented in these pages.

As you read this, fasten your seat belt! This is a no-holds-barred, not-R-rated, but God-rated fabulous adventure into the ultimate relationship between man and woman — the way God planned it, *One Flesh*.

Phil Driscoll
Mighty Horn Ministries
Nashville, Tennessee

One of the best books on marriage!

Bob Yandian's *One Flesh* is one of the best books on marriage I have ever read.

Whether you're single or married, your life will be a lot happier if you follow Bob's direction in this book!

Ray Mossholder
Marriage Plus Ministries
Chatsworth, California

The Bible teaches that sex is here to stay!

The Bible teaches that sex is here to *stay*. Today's culture teaches that sex is for *play*, while sex professionals insist that sex is for *pay*. Currently in our society, the first sexual experiences happen at age ten or eleven. More and more people seek sex in homosexual or lesbian relationships. Our society has become sexually ill.

It does not seem that the answer to today's low moral standard is simply preaching against the *wrongs*. We need good sound teaching on what is *right*. Bob Yandian does this extremely well in *One Flesh*. This book is scriptural, sound and arresting. He has filled its pages with inspiration, instruction and examples to which we can all relate. This book should be required reading for all married couples!

Judson Cornwall
Phoenix, Arizona

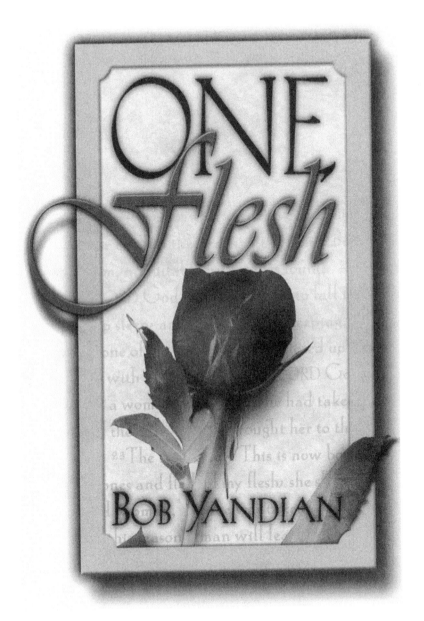

ONE Flesh

BOB YANDIAN

CHARISMA HOUSE

ONE FLESH by Bob Yandian
Published by Charisma House
Charisma Media/Charisma House Book Group
600 Rinehart Road
Lake Mary, FL 32746
www.charismahouse.com

Unless otherwise noted, all Scripture quotations are from the
King James Version of the Bible.

Scripture quotations marked AMP are from the Amplified Bible.
Old Testament copyright © 1965, 1987 by the
Zondervan corporation. The Amplified New Testament
copyright © 1954, 1958, 1987 by the Lockman
Foundation. Used by permission.

Scriptures quotations marked NAS are from the New American
Standard Bible. Copyright © 1960, 1962, 1963, 1968, 1971, 1972,
1973, 1975, 1977 by the Lockman Foundation.
Used by permission.

Library of Congress Catalog Card Number: 94-68521
International Standard Book Number: 978-0-88419-380-7

This book was originally published in 1993
by Pillar Books and Publishing, Tulsa, OK.

14 15 16 17 — 33 32 31 30
Printed in the United States of America

To Ken and Donna Stewart, our pastors at the time, who ministered to us late that night in Memphis. They helped us to finally see the gift in each other we had ignored for so long.

ACKNOWLEDGMENTS

Special thanks go to Tim and Beverly LaHaye for their book *The Act of Marriage*. This is the one book that was so instrumental in turning my attitude toward Loretta around. Although the book was written years ago, I still consider it to be the best. Truth never gets old!

CONTENTS

FOREWORD

Marriage is not what is depicted in fiction, songs or movies. You don't fall in love and live happily ever after without a lot of hard work and give-and-take. Once you *fall* in love, everything doesn't just *fall* into place. It takes knowledge and a willingness to work to make a good, strong and secure marriage.

This book has come from just that way of life. We entered into marriage with the idea of fireworks and everything going smoothly.

It didn't take us long to discover that was not the way things worked! So we began to apply ourselves to wisdom and understanding. It took a lot of blood, sweat and tears, but in the end the rewards were wonderful.

Hopefully, you are either not married or just beginning your marriage, and you will be able to avoid some of the pitfalls. However, even if you have been married a very long time and feel there is no hope of redeeming your marriage, let me tell you it is never too late, and God will redeem the time!

I know you will receive comfort, wisdom and understanding as you read this book.

Loretta Yandian

INTRODUCTION

One of the greatest Christian witnesses to the world today is a happy, productive marriage. Believers' marriages should be living proof to unbelievers that Jesus Christ heals families, brings husbands and wives together and enables them to repulse sin and live godly lives. The Bible says you are an "epistle...known and read of all men" (2 Corinthians 3:2), and your marriage is a major part of your "letter" to those around you.

Unfortunately, Christians have been notorious for having

some of the worst marriages. Many unbelievers' marriages are better than some Christian marriages. The divorce rate in the Church is almost as high as the world's, and often the marriages you think are just fantastic are having the worst time. People in our local churches can put up tremendous facades to hide their problems.

The truth is that Christian marriages ought to be the best. If two people have accepted the Lord and are following the Holy Spirit, there should be no reason for them to get a divorce. Furthermore, they should be able to rise above the struggle, stay together and come to a place of peace and joy in their relationship.

> For the grace of God that *bringeth salvation* hath appeared to all men, *teaching us* that, denying ungodliness and worldly lusts, we should live soberly, righteously, and godly, in this present world (Titus 2:11-12, italics added).

The grace of God brings us salvation, which means healing, deliverance and soundness in *all* areas of our lives, including marriage. Verse 12 also says that the grace of God is a teacher. His grace teaches us how to live like Jesus Christ in this earth. We can be witnesses to those who are lost that the gospel can supernaturally transform their lives, resolve their marriage problems and restore their families.

Most Christian couples don't realize that through godly counsel, studying the Word of God and praying together, they can be *taught* to have a successful and happy marriage relationship. They read Titus 2:11-12 and appropriate the promises of God for their *eternal* life, but it never occurs to them that the promises of God are for all areas of their *natural* life as well.

I think one of the main reasons Christians get divorced is because they don't come for church counsel until it is too late. The devil convinces them that their problems are

13

unique, or the trouble they are having is just too "dirty" to bring to a church counselor. But we are going to find out from the Bible that there are no new problems, there are no unsolvable problems, and the "dirty" problems are more prevalent in the Church than most Christians would think.

Satan is the same yesterday, today and forever, and the difficulties in marriage are the same as well. However, so are God's solutions to those difficulties.

If a couple will set everything aside and seek God together before a problem area becomes too overwhelming, or go for Bible-based counsel if the conflict is too great to settle themselves, they can overcome their differences and stop the enemy from gaining a stronghold in their relationship.

Recently, I heard the startling statistic that in one out of three marriages in America today, one of the partners has been married at least once before. Children are having to decide which parent they will spend their holidays with. One article I read said that by the year 2000 there would be less traditional family life and more "alternative family lifestyles" of homosexual and lesbian households.

It is the Church's responsibility to hold up the banner of God's Word and live godly lives in an ungodly world. I don't care what society says, what the "new world order" says or what any "expert" says, because *God teaches that the family is the foundation of a society.* Whatever happens to the family will happen to the nation. More than that, the family is the fundamental organization on which each local church and ultimately the universal Church is built.

People always ask me, "What's your vision for your church?" My vision is simple: I want to see stable, dependable Christians who are passionate about the things of God and compassionate toward one another. Nothing upsets me more than to hear Christians use God as an excuse for not keeping their word, not paying their bills, not walking in morality or not living up to their responsibilities to their families.

The Bible is not "so spiritually minded that it is no earthly good." God is practical as well as spiritual. He operates in both realms, and believers ought to operate in both realms also. Some believers get so practical they become carnal; others become so spiritual they can't relate to anyone or keep a job.

God is completely balanced as He operates in both the spiritual realm and the natural realm. He can knock you over with His power and carry you away in His presence one day, then tell you how to perform a specific, even trivial task on the job the next day.

God doesn't tell you one thing one minute and the opposite the next; He isn't up one day and down the next. He is dependable. His Word is absolutely true, and His Spirit is steadfast. I believe He wants His children to be true, dependable and steadfast as well. Our word should be as good on Tuesday as it is on Sunday!

My greatest hope and dream is to see the Body of Christ live their lives with such love and integrity that people will stop them and ask, "What's different about you? Your family is so dependable, so stable and so happy all the time." What a witness to this immoral, insecure and hopeless world!

Then the believers can answer, "It is Jesus Christ who has made the difference in our lives. Would you like to know Him, too?" The condition of a believer's marriage and family life is a powerful daily witness to unsaved relatives, neighbors, co-workers and friends.

I praise God for the members of my congregation who receive the Word of God and live it before the world. I've found that the ones who are really walking the walk and not just talking the talk are the ones whose personal lives are consistently growing in stability and being filled with joy.

When I taught this series at our church, I saw many impossible situations turned around by the teaching of the

Word and the Spirit of God, and the tape series has always been one of my best-selling series across the nation and around the world. It is my prayer that this book will reach every Christian couple who desperately needs help, as well as those who are doing well but want their marriage to continue getting better.

There is no limit to the joy, pleasure and blessing God can bring to you through a marriage in which you and your spouse are truly *One Flesh*. ❧

ONE

IN THE BEGINNING THERE WAS GODLY PASSION

WHEN I met my wife, Loretta, we knew almost immediately that we were right for one another. Although we dated for a year before we were married, we really didn't know much about marriage. We thought that when two people were married, everything would come naturally, and they would just know what to do in any given situation.

Somehow I would automatically know how to be the head of the home, and she would know how to submit to my authority. Everything would just flow, and our love would get stronger and stronger. Then one day we would have kids, and by some innate knowledge we would also know how to raise them. Certainly, because God brought us together and we were living for Him, everything else would fall into place.

We were in for a big surprise!

Ignorance Is Not Bliss!

Titus 2:1-8 tells us it is necessary for the older men and women to teach the younger men and women how to conduct themselves in life, including how to be godly husbands and fathers or wives and mothers. These skills are *learned* — we are not born with all the knowledge and wisdom we need concerning family life.

Because I was studying for the ministry, I thought our family life would be perfect. After all, we were serving the Lord, but we had one of the most miserable marriages! It never occurred to me that I had to study and meditate on what the Word of God had to say about marriage and raising children. I needed to put God's promises into action in order to have a good marriage just the way that I acted on His promises in order to receive guidance or healing. A successful spiritual life — or marriage — is not mainte-nance free.

I finally realized how ignorant I was about marriage and family life when my wife was ready to walk out the door and I had no objection. Our marriage was a failure, and we both knew it. The only reason we did not divorce, and the only reason we have the tremendous marriage we have today, is that we both agreed to wise up. We dedicated ourselves to finding out what God's intention for marriage was and then changing ourselves — not each other — to conform to His blueprint.

The result was that Loretta and I grew more in love with

each other than we ever imagined we could—even more than we imagined when we first met and fell in love. More than that, we have become the best of friends. Instead of being a painful burden, our marriage has become a refuge of love, joy and comfort.

In this book you will study some of the same foundational Scripture selections we have studied and trusted in to keep our marriage on track with God. At the same time I will be sharing the practical application of these scriptures — and some good common sense that we have picked up over the years as well.

The place to begin, of course, is in the book of Genesis. Here, God instituted marriage in the Garden of Eden, and we discover its original framework.

In God's Image

The first two chapters of Genesis contain the Bible's account of creation. In these chapters the Holy Spirit tells us everything God created and when He created it. Even most unbelievers know that Genesis 1:1 reads, "In the beginning God created the heaven and the earth."

We don't know exactly when "the beginning" was, but it was a long time ago. Although the Bible tells us the earth is very old (Hebrews 1:10-12), we know that man was put on this earth approximately six thousand years ago. It just so happened that man was the last creature God created. He created the perfect environment for mankind before He created man.

On the sixth and final day of creation, God created all the animals, and then He created man. Even though man is an entirely different species from any other living creature, his body was formed of the dust of the earth just as the animals' bodies were (Genesis 2:7). However, there were major differences between man and the other animals, the primary one being that man was made in God's image.

> And God said, Let us make man in our image,
> after our likeness: and let them have dominion
> over the fish of the sea, and over the fowl of the
> air, and over the cattle, and over all the earth, and
> over every creeping thing that creepeth upon the
> earth (Genesis 1:26).

We know that God does not have a physical, flesh-and-blood body. The Bible makes it clear that He is a Spirit (John 4:24). However, even spirit beings have form, and God is not a cloud floating around that disintegrates and rematerializes. I believe when we get to heaven and actually see Him sitting on His throne, He will have the form of a man.

We know God has a form like our physical form from many verses of Scripture. Psalm 44:3 says, "Thy right hand, and thine arm, and the light of thy countenance." This passage refers to God's hand, His arm and His facial expression. In Lamentations 1:15 we read, "The Lord hath trodden under foot," and in Matthew 5:35 Jesus states that the earth is God's footstool.

One of the most striking passages of Scripture referring to the form of God is found in Exodus 33:22-23, in which Moses asks to see God's glory. God answers his request as follows:

> And it shall come to pass, while my glory passeth
> by, that I will put thee in a clift of the rock, and
> will cover thee with my hand while I pass by:
> And I will take away mine hand, and thou shalt
> see my back parts: but my face shall not be seen.

In the Bible, whenever the spirits of people who had died appeared, they appeared in human bodily form. For example, when the spirits of Elijah and Moses appeared on the Mount of Transfiguration with Jesus (Matthew 17:3), they looked like their physical bodies had looked when they were alive on earth.

So we can see that not only was man's spirit made in the image of God, but man's body was formed from the dust of the earth to look like the *form* of God. As we take a closer look at Genesis 1:26-27, we see a description of both the making of man's body and the creating of his spirit. Both are formed in the image of God.

Something Out of Nothing

The Bible says in Genesis 1:26, "Let us *make* man in our image," and in verse 27, "So God *created* man in his own image." The words I have italicized are translated differently because they are two different Hebrew words. In verse 26, the word for "make" is *asah,* which means "to *manufacture* something out of *something.*" In verse 27, the word for "create" is *bara,* which means "to *create* something out of *nothing.*" [1] The King James Version translates *asah* as "made" and *bara* as "created."

Because man's body was formed from the dust of the ground, from something which already existed, his body was *asah* (made). But the spirit of man was *bara* (created). The spirit of man had no origin, and it was not made out of anything that previously existed. God *created* the spirit of the man.

When a person is conceived in the womb, their body comes from preexisting material, formed from the union of the sperm of the man and the egg of the woman. But their spirit is created (*bara*) supernaturally by God at the moment of conception. When the physical form of a human being begins, the spirit of that person is implanted into the embryo. The miracle of conception is not only in the formation of a child's body, but in the creation of a brand-new human spirit who will live forever, even after their body has perished.

The spirit of man and the form of man are what separate him from the animal kingdom. Man is the only creature God made who possesses an eternal spirit and who is created in the image of Himself. Unlike plants and animals, people have an eternal existence because they are spirit beings. Receiving Jesus merely determines that they will spend eternity in the presence of God (eternal life) rather than separated from God (eternal death).

> And the Lord God formed man of the dust of the ground, and breathed into his nostrils the breath of life; and man became a living soul (Genesis 2:7).

This verse calls man a "living soul." The soul is the part of man that contains his mind, emotions and will. The term *living soul* means that the soul of man is eternal because it is contained within a spirit that is eternal. Animals have souls. They have personalities, a degree of reasoning and thinking ability, and emotions. However, they are not spirit beings, so they are not "living" souls. While they are alive, they have no consciousness of eternity because they do not possess an eternal spirit.

The uniqueness of man is that he is made in the image of God, and he instinctively knows he will live forever. His soul, his personality, his character and the content of his life on earth are eternal. They are contained within his spirit, which was created (*bara*) by God at conception.

Male and Female

Have you ever wondered why Genesis 1:27 says, "So God created [*bara*] man in his own image, in the image of God created [*bara*] he *him;* male and female created [*bara*] he *them*"? Why does the Holy Spirit mention *him* and then mention *them?* Because inside of *him* was *them.*

Immediately you might ask, Is the Bible saying that inside of him were two bodies? No! In verse 27 the word used for "create" is *bara*, which means to create something out of nothing. This verse is talking about the creation of their *spirits*, not the making of their bodies.

Taking another look at Genesis 2:7, it says that God formed man from the dust and then "breathed into his nostrils the breath of life." The word *life* is actually plural, *lives*. God breathed into the body of the man the "breath of lives." After God made the body of the man from the dust of the earth, He breathed into the body of the man the created spirits of both the man and the woman.

This man was not a freak or a bisexual, nor was he two people trapped in one body. He was one human male body containing within himself the spiritual essence of male and female. God created him whole and complete in himself.

> Male and female created [*bara*] he them; and blessed them, and called their name Adam, in the day when they were created [*bara*] (Genesis 5:2).

We know Adam's body and Eve's body were not created on the same day. God created Adam's body on the sixth day and then rested on the seventh. We do not know how long after the seventh day it was before He put the man to sleep, took the spirit and soul of the woman out of the man and formed her body from his rib (Genesis 2:21-22).

The "male and female" which God created on the sixth day, the day He made (*asah*) Adam's body, were the created (*bara*) spirits of Adam and Eve. Then, sometime after Adam had completed naming all the creatures of the garden, the Bible says:

> The Lord God caused a deep sleep to fall upon Adam, and he slept: and he took one of his ribs,

and closed up the flesh instead thereof; and the rib, which the Lord God had taken from man, made he a woman (Genesis 2:21-22).

It was more than a rib that God took out of Adam; He pulled out the spirit and soul of Eve. He used the rib to manufacture her body, but her spirit already existed, having been created when God created Adam's spirit.

A Glorious Analogy

At this point you are probably wondering, "Why did God choose to create man and woman in such a bizarre fashion?" The manner in which God chose to make the bodies and create the spirits of Adam and Eve is a type and shadow of Jesus and the Church.

In His foreknowledge, God knew Adam would sin. He also knew He would one day send Jesus to pay the price for that sin. Therefore, in order to instruct man, everything God established in the Old Testament — the law, the sacrifices and even the one-flesh relationship in marriage — are symbols of the redemptive work of the Lord Jesus Christ.

The way that God made Adam and Eve, took Eve out of Adam, and then brought her back to him is a type of Jesus and the Church.

In 1 Corinthians 15:45 Jesus is called "the last Adam," which means He entered this earth outside of the curse. There was a time when Jesus walked this earth and was complete. He carried the Church within Himself because we were chosen in Christ before the foundation of the world (Ephesians 1:4).

Jesus carried the spirit and soul of the Church inside Him. When He went to the cross, His side was opened up. On Pentecost, God began to build the Body of Christ from the rib of Jesus (120 disciples in the upper room), and it is still being built today (Matthew 16:18).

Just as God presented Eve to Adam, the day is coming very quickly when the Bride of Christ will be completed. God the Father will present her, a glorious church without spot or wrinkle, to the Lord Jesus Christ (Ephesians 5:27). Jesus is anxiously awaiting that day because then He will be complete again — what was taken out of Him will return to Him!

The Institution of Marriage

Marriage was instituted before man fell and before the plan of redemption was executed. The significance of God's timing is this: The institution of marriage applies to the whole human race. Whether people are believers or unbelievers, God has instituted the joy and pleasure of marriage for all mankind. That is why many unbelievers have great marriages.

Solomon knew God, but he was never happily married. Oddly enough, he observed how many unbelievers had good marriages.

> Live joyfully with the wife whom thou lovest all the days of the life of thy vanity [apart from God], which he hath given thee under the sun, all the days of thy vanity: *for that is thy portion in this life,* and in thy labour which thou takest under the sun (Ecclesiastes 9:9, italics added).

Solomon observed that the only heaven on earth unbelievers will ever know is the experience of a good marriage. God instituted marriage for happiness before the fall of man; therefore, even without receiving Jesus as Lord of their lives, a couple can still enjoy a good marriage.

God designed marriage as a refuge for times when everything is going wrong in the world, when people don't like you or when you're facing problems. Ideally, your marriage partner is someone who loves you and cares for you regardless of what is going on around you or what you are going through. Your partner is there to help you solve your problems and provide security in a world that is constantly changing.

Solomon says that marriage is a blessing that even an unbeliever can enjoy, but notice that he qualifies this by adding, "in thy *labour* which thou takest under the sun." Unbelievers who have good marriages have discovered that the secret is labor! This is why some unbelievers have marriages that are more successful than those of some believers. Marriage is only as good as the degree to which the couple is willing to work at it, and many believers are not willing to pay the price for a successful marriage.

The Woman

Meanwhile, back in the Garden of Eden.... God is very practical, and He knew exactly how to prepare Adam for Eve. It is interesting to note the sequence of events leading to the time when He put Adam to sleep.

> And the Lord God said, It is not good that the man should be alone; I will make him an help meet for him. And out of the ground the Lord God formed every beast of the field, and every fowl of the air; and brought them unto Adam to see what he would call them: and whatsoever Adam called every living creature, that was the name thereof.
>
> And Adam gave names to all cattle, and to the fowl of the air, and to every beast of the field; but for Adam there was not found an help meet for him (Genesis 2:18-20).

As Adam named every species on the earth, a picture was being pounded into his mind: God created every species

26

as male and female in bodily form. He did not create one
elephant, one bird or one salmon, or else those species
would have ceased to exist after the first generation.

Imagine Adam standing there in the Garden of Eden as
God paraded all the animals, two by two, in front of him.
Perhaps for days, weeks, months or even years Adam stood
there and named all the creatures, male and female. All of
them came in pairs, until finally God had made His point:
"Adam, you are just one, and all the others are two. It is not
good for man to be alone, so I'm going to give you a
partner like yourself."

> And the Lord God caused a deep sleep to fall
> upon Adam, and he slept: and he took one of his
> ribs, and closed up the flesh instead thereof; and
> the rib, which the Lord God had taken from man,
> made he a woman, and brought her unto the
> man. And Adam said, This is now bone of my
> bones, and flesh of my flesh: she shall be called
> Woman, because she was taken out of Man
> (Genesis 2:21-23).

In order to see how special the woman is in creation, we
need to look again at how God formed the body of the
man. Genesis 2:7 says God "formed" the man from the dust
of the ground. The Hebrew word for "formed" is *yatsar,*
which means "to form, mold or shape." This word is used
throughout the Old Testament to describe how a potter
molds and forms his clay.

So the man's body was *asah*, made from something that
already existed (Genesis 1:26), and also *yatsar,* molded and
formed like a lump of clay. Remember also, the animals
were all *yatsar,* molded and formed from the dust of the
ground — both male *and female* of every species.

In the animal kingdom, the female of each species was
independently made from the dust in the same way the

male was made. *But God made the woman in an entirely different manner than He made the man or any other creature.* He put Adam to sleep so He could perform the world's first major surgery, removing not only the rib, but the spirit and soul of Eve from Adam's body.

The Bible doesn't say how long Adam was asleep. We often think of him as being unconscious for an hour or two, but the Hebrew words used to describe the making of Eve indicate that God took His time when He made her. Adam could have slept for a long time!

> And the rib, which the Lord God had taken from man, made he a woman (Genesis 2:22).

In this verse we have a different word from *asah* (to make something from something), *bara* (to create something from nothing) and *yatsar* (to mold, form or shape something). The Hebrew word translated "made" here is *banah*, which means "to build something."

God took the rib in His hands, supernaturally multiplied it and constructed it into the body of the woman. Just as the loaves and fishes multiplied in the hands of Jesus (John 6:5-14), God multiplied the rib and built it, piece by piece, into the form of Eve. The man and all the other creatures were molded from the dust of the ground, but the woman was *built.* (We still use that term today!)

There's Nothing Like a Dame

God took His time when He made the body of the woman, because she was going to be gorgeous! Unlike the creatures in nature, in which the male is the more beautiful, the female of the species of man was going to be the beautiful one. In nature the male is often the one who lies around and primps while the female gets the food and does all the work.

In mankind, God ordained that the woman be the exquisite one for whom the man provides and whom he protects.

God took His time with the woman in order to make her different from any other creature. He made her so that man would take one look at her and his eyes would pop out of his head. I believe that is why He had Adam name all the animals first, because after Adam saw Eve, he would not be able to keep his mind on his work! As fascinating and wonderful as all the different creatures of the earth were to him, none of them had the impact on him that Eve was going to have.

Again, God didn't cause a light sleep to fall on Adam. He caused a deep sleep to fall on him because He needed him to be out for a while. God needed time to build this totally unique creature. She was different from all the females of every other species because her body was not made separately from the male nor was it composed of the dust of the ground. Her body was constructed from part of the man's body.

Woman was taken out of the man, which symbolizes that she draws her life from the man. She was then returned to the man, which represents how she gives his life back to him.

When Adam saw Eve, he said:

> This is now bone of my bones, and flesh of my flesh: she shall be called Woman, because she was taken out of Man (Genesis 2:23).

The very name *woman* speaks of her being drawn from the man. *That is why there is a spiritual bond and a sense of morality between a husband and wife that no other species of nature experiences.*

Did you ever consider the fact that in the animal kingdom there is no such thing as sexual immorality? Very few animals mate for life. Most have many mates everywhere, and they don't feel guilty after they have sex with any number of their own kind. We often refer to somebody as having "the morals of an alley cat" because cats have those morals. They were created that way. But man and woman were designed to have an entirely different sexual relationship than animals.

One Rib Means One Woman

When God took the rib out of Adam, He took one rib, not two or three or more. Adam didn't wake up and see five women standing in front of him. Nor did God give him seven women — one woman for every day of the week. God ordained one woman for one man. And the woman completes the man as nothing else in creation can. A relationship exists between husband and wife that is not found anywhere else in creation.

Because God ordained one woman for one man, when a person practices sexual promiscuity, in which a physical union is formed with many different people, the soul and body enter into confusion. Anyone who believes they can enjoy sexual relations with more than one person and shake it off as some superficial part of their life is in confusion.

In the Garden of Eden, God established a spiritual bond between husband and wife which is the basis for all sexual morality and purity. When sexual fidelity is practiced, the marriage will bring peace and prosperity to the home. When it is violated, confusion and misery will reign.

In societies where promiscuity is practiced, the results are obvious — families are torn apart, lives are broken and disoriented, and physical diseases directly related to sexual immorality run rampant. First Corinthians 6:18 tells us that the only sin that directly affects our body is sexual sin.

Today we watch in horror as millions are dying terrible deaths from AIDS, which is just one of many sexually transmitted diseases that are growing out of control. The Bible tells us this catastrophe can be prevented by adhering to God's rules regarding sex. Yet man continues to put himself in jeopardy by going his own way. Men and women risk death for a few minutes of sexual gratification. This is ultimate confusion.

The Old Testament Polygamists

One question comes up every time I teach that God ordained one woman for one man: What about the fact that the Bible records many instances of polygamy (being married to more than one wife) in the Old Testament? The Mormons, who still practice polygamy today, defend their way of life by quoting Scripture passages about Jacob, David and many others who had more than one wife.

But if you study their lives carefully, it will be obvious that confusion reigned in the households of those who had more than one wife. Furthermore, both the Old and New Testaments make it clear that this was not God's will.

The first recorded case of polygamy is in Genesis 4:19, where a man named Lamech took more than one wife. We find out later, in verse 23, that he was a murderer. So the first polygamist recorded in the Bible was a murderer!

Jacob was the first Jew to have more than one wife. He worked for seven years to get Rachel and was tricked into marrying her sister Leah, so he worked another seven years to get Rachel as well. Needless to say, the two wives fought constantly, jealousy and strife existed between them and their children, and Jacob always had trouble in the home. Eventually the sons of Leah tried to kill Joseph, one of the sons of Rachel.

First Samuel 1:1-6 records the account of Elkanah, who had two wives, Peninnah and Hannah. As you remember, Hannah was not able to have children, and Peninnah, who had given Elkanah many children, constantly insulted and harassed Hannah because she was barren. When Samuel was finally born to Hannah, the insults about being barren may have stopped, but the strife and jealousy most likely did not.

Under Moses, God set the record straight when He gave the Law. Leviticus 18:18 and Deuteronomy 17:17 are two verses of Scripture which make it clear that a man should not have more than one wife. Later, David broke this law. When he met Bathsheba, he already had five wives. The Bible doesn't say anything about strife among the wives, but his children committed incest, tried to kill one another and even attempted to overthrow David from his throne.

David and Bathsheba's son Solomon out-married everyone else, having had seven hundred wives and three hundred concubines. If there is any question about the destruction Solomon's promiscuity and sexual sin brought to his life, I believe it will be answered in chapters 2 and 3 of this book. No one was more miserable and dissipated because of sexual immorality than Solomon.

The New Testament explicitly tells us there is to be one woman for one man and one man for one woman. Never in the entire Word of God do you read, "Husband, love your wives." We're told in 1 Timothy 3:2 that a bishop should be the husband of one wife, and verse 12 gives the same qualification for the office of deacon. This is confirmed again in Titus 1:6, which says that elders should be the husband of one wife.

Since marriage is a type of Jesus and the Church, we can take this one step further and ask, "How many bodies does Jesus Christ have?" The answer is one. Jesus is coming back for one Church, one Body. Jesus is called the Bridegroom, and the Church is called the Bride — one Bride for one Bridegroom.

Moreover, how many bodies do you have? You have one. There is one body for one head. You would look really strange if you had more than one body under your head —

or more than one head on top of your body! Bodies such as these are freaks in nature, and they are against what God has ordained for mankind in marriage as well.

Throughout the Bible the cornerstone of the family is the one-flesh, one-man-for-one-woman marriage relationship.

The Significance of the Rib

God took one rib from Adam and made one woman for him from that rib. A great deal of wrong teaching and misapplication of this passage of Scripture comes when people try to make more out of the rib than what it is. For years women have been offended when they were identified as just a rib from the man. But only the woman's body was constructed from the rib. Her spirit and soul were complete before her body was ever made.

The Hebrew word for "rib" — *tsalah* — means exactly what it says, a rib from a physical skeleton. In the book of Daniel, a beast is spoken of that rose up and devoured other beasts. Daniel saw the ribs of the devoured beasts in the mouth of the first beast. This is the same word *rib* (Daniel 7:5).

However, in 1 Kings 6 and 7 there is a description of all the houses Solomon built, including the house of the Lord. Here the same word translated "rib" in Genesis 2:22 is translated "beam" (1 Kings 7:3). Hidden within the structures that Solomon built were beams (ribs) that supported them.

No matter how magnificent a building looks from the outside, without the hidden beams holding it up, it would collapse and fall to the ground as rubble — and the same is true for the man. The world sees a man's tough facade, the businessman exterior, the wisdom and strength he wields at the office or in his profession. But his wife is the hidden beam who knows the little boy on the inside of him!

She knows what he's really like, what his strengths and

weaknesses are, and she's the hidden support of his life. Other than the Lord, she is the most important thing in his life. Without her, he is like a building without beams to uphold it, and his life would collapse.

Many men try to promote the idea that they are independent, that they could easily live without their wives. I've spoken with women who say that their husbands act as though they don't exist. "He behaves as though I could walk out the door and his life would go right on as usual. All he needs is someone to cook, clean, take care of the kids and have sex with him, and he can find anyone to do that."

I have something to say to these men: The day she walks out is the day you fold! It is very significant that God took Adam's rib to build the woman. Without ribs, not only would the body collapse, but the heart would be vulnerable. *The rib represents emotional support, the hidden, inward strength and encouragement without which you would fall apart.*

My congregation sees me, their pastor, week after week, preaching and teaching with great confidence. They see the stability in my life that enables me to carry out the vision God has given me for our church. They see the joy that goes along with doing what God has called me to do.

What they don't see are the times I go home and fall apart, and my wife is there to pick me up, to encourage me, to point me back to the wisdom and strength found only in God. She is the hidden strength of my life. I know without a doubt that the success of my life and ministry rest not only in my relationship with God, but in my relationship with her.

It is very important for a wife to understand that being the hidden support for her husband is a sacred trust. The rib is not visible; it covers the heart because the confidences of her husband are not for public knowledge. If a wife continuously reveals private conversations with her husband to friends, their marriage will be jeopardized. Her husband must be able to trust her with his heart. (This principle of privacy and trust applies to the husband as well. A wife needs to know she can count on her husband to keep her confidences.)

The rib is positioned under the man's arm, which symbolizes the protection and provision the husband gives his wife. God did not take a bone from Adam's foot, because Eve was not to be a slave; nor did He take a bone from his head, because she was not to rule over him either. He took a rib from man's side because she is to stand beside him as his equal before God, to love him, support him, work with him, counsel him, honor him as her protector and provider, and cherish him as her most intimate friend and lover.

Godly Passion

When God took the rib from Adam, the Hebrew language indicates that He did it quickly and violently. He reached in and yanked Eve out. Then, when He brought Eve to Adam, the Hebrew indicates it was just as dramatic a moment. Adam opened his eyes, saw this incredible creature standing before him and immediately recognized her as part of himself. She was different from the animals of the garden. Her bones were made from his bones; her spirit and her soul had been taken out of him.

> And Adam said, This is now bone of my bones, and flesh of my flesh: she shall be called Woman, because she was taken out of Man (Genesis 2:23).

There is a godly passion that is almost violently overpowering when a man and a woman realize they are right for one another and that God has sovereignly and supernaturally brought them together. They suddenly possess one another; they are filled with thoughts of one another, and everything they do is wrapped up in each other.

Initially, when Adam awoke, I imagine he felt a lot different from how he had ever felt before. Something vital, a living part of himself, was missing. For the first time in his life he felt incomplete where he had been complete before. He may have felt empty inside and even lonely for the one who had been a part of him.

Then God said to him, "Adam, get up and splash some cold water on your face because I have one more creature for you to name," and He brought Eve to him. Adam knew her at once, because her spirit and soul had dwelt inside him. He was excited to see her, not only because she looked good on the outside, but because his spirit and soul reached out to her spirit and soul.

This establishes a principle in relationships between men and women that is of the utmost importance: *Adam knew, loved and had intimate knowledge of Eve's spirit and soul before he ever became intimate with her body.*

He had already discovered her uniqueness and how to love her, protect her and keep her. They had built a foundation of understanding and trust. Then, when God brought her to him in her physical body, she could freely give herself to him, and he could freely trust and delight in her.

We live in a culture where the emphasis in relationships is placed upon the body. The body is worshipped and glorified in posters and magazines, on television and in movies. In recent years the world has become fanatical about exercise, and eating disorders and diet fads touch nearly every household. People will even undergo all kinds of surgery to look the way they believe they have to look to feel good about themselves and to attract the kind of person they think is attractive. Desirability is totally wrapped up in the physical appearance.

But the Bible teaches that, although bodily exercise might profit a little in this life, developing the soul and spirit reaps an eternal reward (1 Timothy 4:8). So we can see another major reason why God created Adam and Eve in this unusual way: *God created the spirit and soul of Eve long before He made her body because He wanted to establish the order of how relationships should progress.*

Put Out the Unholy Fire

Again, as we study the passage of Scripture where Adam and Eve come together physically, we see how there is a tremendous passion that burns between a man and a woman who know they are right for one another. God has brought them together, and they will be married, committed to and in covenant with one another until one or both of them dies. This is godly passion.

Godly passion is righteous and holy because it is a reflection of the passionate, unconditional and all-consuming love that God has for His children and that Jesus has for the Church. The perversion of this gift is self-centered lust.

Like godly passion, lust burns within the heart as a raging fire, but it brings destruction instead of wholeness. Where godly passion between a husband and wife brings lasting joy and peace, lust is a fire within that tears down souls and reduces lives to ashes. Godly passion is motivated by selflessness and unconditional love; lust is a hard-driving force that is motivated by selfishness and physical impulses. In simple terms, godly passion gives; lust takes.

> Can a man take fire in his bosom, and his clothes
> not be burned? Can one go upon hot coals, and
> his feet not be burned? (Proverbs 6:27-28).

These verses describe the exact opposite of godly passion. Like godly passion, the fire of lust begins on the inside, in the soul, but it generally involves thoughts of sexual immorality. If these thoughts and consequent emotions are allowed to continue and grow, they will eventually manifest in sexual deeds. The fire in the bosom will eventually work its way out to burn the clothes!

The Word of God instructs us to extinguish the fire of lust on the inside so it cannot work its way to the outside to destroy our lives. Don't try to understand it; flee it (2 Timothy 2:22)! Throw the water of the Word of God on this unholy fire as soon as you recognize it (2 Peter 1:4; 2 Corinthians 10:5).

Don't give lust any power over your thoughts, your feelings or your will. If you do not stop it in its tracks, if you allow it to rule your life, then it will be as if you are walking on hot coals. Your feet will get burned!

Your walk with the Lord and your relationship with your spouse will be hindered and distorted if you continue to indulge in sexual immorality, whether in thought or deed (Proverbs 6:28). You cannot freely fellowship with God or your mate, and live with them in total honesty and trust, if your soul is on fire with self-centered lust.

Each of us has days when lust is a problem. The world does not make it any easier with its billboards, television, magazines and movies that promote immoral thinking and actions with regard to sex. The world seeks to channel a God-given desire in the wrong direction.

Everyone has evil thoughts come to them from time to time, but sin occurs only when you continue to entertain these thoughts instead of turning from them to the Word of God. The earlier you train your children to handle the sex drive, and the faster you as an adult commit yourself to resist the sin of lust, the easier it will be to stay pure until marriage and to remain faithful once you are married.

The way any believer, whether young or old, handles these strong physical drives is the same way a believer avoids all sin. The psalmist wrote:

> Thy word have I hid in mine heart, that I might not sin against thee (Psalms 119:11).

God's Word will give you patience and faith to wait for the right mate to come along, and the Holy Spirit will also give you supernatural strength to keep your sex drive under control.

And just because you are older or married does not mean your sex drive is always under control. Even when you are married, lust tries to rule your heart. There is a temptation to take advantage of your spouse, to use him or her to fulfill a carnal, self-centered desire or an immoral fantasy. If you do not resist this temptation, you will be taking from instead of giving to your mate.

All of us have a battle with our flesh, regardless of age or whether we are single or married. Every believer must keep himself pure in thought, word and deed, walking in love by the application of the Scriptures.

> That by these [exceeding great and precious promises] ye might be partakers of the divine nature, having escaped the corruption that is in the world through lust (2 Peter 1:4).

This verse tells us that when we turn our thoughts to God's Word, we partake of "the divine nature." Literally, we are appropriating the power and holiness of God for our minds and hearts. Through His strength, we can defeat temptation and lead a fulfilled life. Our best example is Jesus in Luke 4. When He was tempted by the devil, He immediately turned to Scripture. He showed us how to be more than conquerors!

One Flesh

> She shall be called Woman, because she was taken out of Man (Genesis 2:23).

In the blaze of godly passion, Adam named the woman.

He named her in a unique way — after himself. This was not a self-centered act of egotism; rather it reflected the nature of their intimate relationship. In the Hebrew it reads, "she shall be called *Ishshah*, because she was taken out of *Ish*."

> Therefore shall a man leave his father and his mother, and shall *cleave* unto his wife: and they shall be one flesh (Genesis 2:24, italics added).

The translators of the King James Version probably didn't know what to do with the Hebrew word for "cleave," because it literally means "sexual intercourse." I believe they tried to find a word that wouldn't offend anyone because the Hebrew word used here, *dabaq*, literally means "to be joined to."

In the New Testament this verse is quoted in Paul's letter to the Ephesians:

> For this cause shall a man leave his father and mother, and shall be *joined* unto his wife, and they two shall be one flesh (Ephesians 5:31, italics added).

The Hebrew word for sex in the Old Testament was translated as "cleave," and the Greek word for sex in the New Testament was translated as "join." The Greek word translated "joined" is *proskollao*, which is an interesting compound word.

Kollao simply means "to be adhered to" and can refer to the physical act of sex. But *pros* indicates a deep intimacy, a face-to-face encounter. When you put the two words together, the Bible is describing the one-flesh relationship between husband and wife.

One flesh involves more than just two individuals having sex. In the act of sex, husband and wife have a relationship, not just a physical experience.

It is significant that man and woman are the only creatures God designed to have sexual intercourse face-to-face. He did not design the animals to have sex facing each other, just as He did not create them with a sense of morality. In the animal kingdom, sex is a natural instinct that exists for the purpose of producing more of the same species (*kollao*). There is no spiritual significance to the sexual act and no "oneness" (*proskollao*) among animals.

> What? know ye not that he which is joined to an harlot is one body? for two, saith he, shall be one flesh (1 Corinthians 6:16).

The Greek word used for "joined" in this verse is just *kollao,* not *proskollao.* The Holy Spirit is letting us know that a man who has sex with a prostitute is just having sex. He is joined with her for the moment, and then it is over. He has added nothing of lasting value to his life; in fact, he has reduced himself to the level of an animal.

What God created to be one of the most fulfilling and beautiful experiences in life, Satan has perverted and exploited. The reason he has tried to distort this gift of God is because becoming "one flesh" with your mate is the closest experience God has given in the natural to the intimate, face-to-face relationship we can have with Him in the spirit.

God ordained sex for marriage as a sacred act and expression of love, faith and trust. The one-flesh experience in marriage, in which your whole life is surrendered to your mate in naked honesty and total trust, gives the greatest pleasure to a man and woman. This is a type of the relationship the Lord desires to have with us spiritually.

Just as our covenant with God through the blood of Jesus Christ is more than a "ticket to heaven," but is a living relationship with our Creator, so is the marriage covenant far more than just a legal and safe way to have sex and produce children. The marriage relationship, as demonstrated

41

in the biblical account of Adam and Eve, is first based on love and understanding between two souls. When you have a strong relationship with your mate's soul, your relationship with your mate's body becomes something fantastic!

All Things Are Honorable in Marriage

A Christian marriage should be conducted with common sense, decency and an understanding of the Word of God in all areas, including sex.

> Marriage is honourable in *all*, and the bed undefiled (Hebrews 13:4, italics added).

The person who translated this verse must have been a monk who knew little about sex! He translated the Greek word *coite* as "bed," but the literal meaning for *coite* is the sex act. From it we get the English word *coitus*. So this verse actually says that the sex act is undefiled in marriage. In plain language, a husband and wife decide together what they believe is right in making love.

What one couple enjoys, another couple may find totally undesirable. One couple's idea of perversion may be another couple's delight. That is why love and respect, not the opinions or preferences of other people, should settle all questions between husband and wife.

Whatever a husband and a wife agree to in the area of sex is not condemned by God when their love toward one another determines the boundaries of their lovemaking. Intimidation or force should never be used by one partner with the other. In such cases, selfish lust has entered into the heart of one or both partners.

In my study of the Word of God, I have been unable to find anything called perversion between a husband and a wife *if they are in agreement.*

Jesus' First Miracle

The Word of God says in Proverbs 5:19 that a husband is to be "ravished" with his wife's love in the act of sex. The Hebrew word used for "ravished" is *shagah,* which literally means to reel from intoxication or to be enraptured. In other words, God wants a husband and wife to be drunk with love for one another! In light of this, I find it even more significant that the first miracle Jesus did was to turn water into wine at the wedding in Cana.

Jesus was doing more than introducing His ministry on earth by performing a miracle. He was also making a statement that marriage is supernatural. The world looks at marriage merely as two people legally living together, but the Bible says that marriage is more than two people co-habiting.

> What therefore God hath joined together, let not man put asunder (Matthew 19:6).

God does not join bodies together — that's the part we do. Jesus did not fill the water pots with water at the wedding in Cana because filling the water pots represented our part in the marriage: coming together in soul and body. He had the servants perform the part that was tangible, that could be *seen.*

God joins spirits together. This is the part that is unseen but every bit as real. When Jesus transformed the water into wine, no one knew it. You couldn't tell from looking at the outside of the water pots that they contained wine. This symbolized the unseen act of God in marriage — the joining of hearts on the inside.

Unbelievers experience a sense of oneness in their souls through sex in marriage, and this oneness can be very fulfilling and may even seem spiritual. But the *spiritual* reality of one flesh can only be experienced by two believers, whose union is intensified and ecstasy increased due to their spiritual union with God.

When a husband and wife are eternally joined to God through Jesus Christ, their one-flesh relationship can explode with the reality of eternal, unconditional love!

You and your mate may look like common water pots to everyone else, but when you come together as one flesh, something miraculous happens — two pots of water become intoxicating wine! This is God's supernatural gift of passion. ⟨⟩

TWO

A FAMOUS FATHER SPEAKS FRANKLY TO HIS SON ABOUT SEX PART ONE: WHAT NOT TO DO

Αll scripture is given by inspiration of God, and is profitable for doctrine [teaching], for reproof, for correction, for instruction in righteousness" (2 Timothy 3:16).

If ever there was a time when the church needed instruction in righteousness, it is now. Sexual misconduct and charges of sexual misconduct seem to plague the Body of Christ more now than ever — or perhaps the modern news media is just more expert in reporting them.

Nevertheless, the only way anyone can avoid or conquer sexual sin is to turn to the Word of God. The best instruction manual on sex is the Bible! Parents should use Scripture to teach their children about sex whenever the subject arises.

The fact that Solomon was taught about sex by his parents, David and Bathsheba, indicates that the proper place for teaching sex is the home. We as Christian parents often complain that the school is not the place to learn about sex, but we fail to instruct our children about it in the framework of the family. This responsibility begins with the father.

King David made a lot of mistakes in his family life, but one of the things he did right was teaching his son Solomon about sex. Several chapters in Proverbs consist of Solomon's account of the instruction his father gave him concerning relationships with women. David was very blunt with Solomon about the pitfalls of sexual immorality, but he was equally frank concerning the sanctity of marriage.

Some of the verses we are about to study will probably cause you to say, "I don't believe this is in the Bible!" And what is even more interesting is knowing David shared these things with Solomon when he was still a boy. We should begin training our children in sexual matters from the precepts of the Scriptures as soon as they show an interest.

You may also be thinking, "But I'm a single adult. I don't need to read about how to tell kids about sex." Wrong! Most adults were never taught about sex from the Bible, and they need to know these things as much as children do.

Wisdom and Understanding

My son, attend unto my wisdom, and bow thine ear to my understanding (Proverbs 5:1).

The term *son* means "builder of the family name." Notice that it does not mean the tearing down of the family name, but the building of the family name. Everything you have built is a foundation for your children, and they should build their lives on the foundation you have given them.

God's plan is that every generation should exceed their parents' generation in excellence. Your children should be even more successful, more prosperous, healthier, bolder in their witness and more skillful in teaching the Word of God than you. When people read about or hear your family name they immediately associate your family with the things of God, as those who follow after God and serve Him faithfully. In every generation, we should be sending wiser, bolder and more godly children into the world.

David knew that Solomon would soon be old enough for his first chariot and that he would cruise through town as the king's son. He knew Solomon would drive by the hang-outs and be exposed to many kinds of girls. To ensure that his son would uphold and build upon the family name instead of tearing it down, David admonished and instructed Solomon about the virtues and pitfalls of sex from God's viewpoint.

In Proverbs 5:1 David is telling Solomon not only to *listen* to his instruction ("attend unto my wisdom") but to *submit* to it ("bow thine ear to my understanding"). It's one thing for a child to listen to what his parents say; it's another thing for him to understand the significance of it and do it. It's the *doing* of truth that passes it down to the next generation.

> That thou mayest regard discretion, and that thy lips may keep knowledge (Proverbs 5:2).

Literally, David is saying that the only way you will be able to exercise discretion, to know what is right and what is wrong, to discern who can be trusted and who cannot, is to submit yourself to the Word of God. You must keep the knowledge of the Scriptures continuously in your mind.

Knowledge of God's Word enables you to discern the character of the people with whom you are dealing in life.

As you line up your life with the wisdom of God, the Holy Spirit in your spirit can communicate to you when something is not right. Or, He can give you peace when you are in God's will but the circumstances are difficult. This is vital information to young — or old — as they are attracted to members of the opposite sex.

David repeats himself to Solomon in Proverbs 6:20-21 when he says:

> My son, keep thy father's commandment, and forsake not the law of thy mother: Bind them continually upon thine heart, and tie them about thy neck.

David's commandment and Bathsheba's law were God's Word. We bind the Word of God upon our hearts and around our necks by meditating on Scripture. Psalm 1 and Joshua 1 both talk about meditating in the Word day and night in order to have a successful, fulfilled life. Children ought to be taught early in life not only to read their Bibles but to meditate, ponder and pray about what they are reading.

Meditating on God's Word is essential for anyone who wants to remain sexually pure.

Every time your child meditates on the Word, God's wisdom and discernment is being bound around his or her heart and neck. When truth is in the heart, the neck cannot be turned by temptation. The Word on the *inside* controls the body on the *outside*.

One day your children will leave your home to live their own lives. This can be a frightening prospect for parents who haven't seen to it that the Word of God is bound around their children's hearts and minds. On the day your children leave home, your imagination can go wild, thinking, "What's going to happen to them without me there to protect them and guide them?"

When that son or daughter goes off to college or gets an apartment and has a job, you may think, "What about all those pretty, worldly girls who will tempt him to compromise? What about the handsome wolves at the office where my sweet, innocent daughter is working? Maybe I should move nearby, or perhaps I should take an office next door in order to protect my children."

But the Bible says if you train them up in the way they should go, if you have taught them to meditate on God's Word and disciplined them to submit to His will, when they are old they will not depart from it (Proverbs 22:6). Notice this verse doesn't say they will not depart from *you* but from *it* — the Word.

When spiritual truth is bound around your children, they will never leave the authority and presence of the Lord. Knowing this you will have peace on the day they leave your authority and presence.

> When thou goest, it shall lead thee; when thou sleepest, it shall keep thee; and when thou awakest, it shall talk with thee (Proverbs 6:22).

This verse says that the Word of God will lead them as they go through their days. When they sleep the Word will guard them, and when they wake up, even if no one is there to say, "Good morning," the Word will speak to them.

Although there comes a day when you cut the apron strings, God never cuts the apron strings! While your children are growing up, while they are still bound to you, you must bind something to them that will never leave them or forsake them — God's Word. That powerful, overriding influence of divine truth and wisdom will give your children discernment and success in life long after they have left home. And when you release them, you will have the peace of mind and confidence that, no matter what they face, they are going to be all right without you.

> For the commandment is a lamp; and the law is light; and reproofs of instruction are the way of life: To keep thee from the evil woman, from the flattery of the tongue of a strange woman (Proverbs 6:23-24).

These verses of Scripture tell why it is so important for our children to be grounded in the Word of God: to keep them from the "evil woman" and the "strange woman." Now if David had been speaking to a daughter, he could just as easily have said, "to keep thee from the evil man and the strange man." The truths that David is passing on to Solomon apply to girls as well as boys, because sexual immorality is a temptation for both.

We have already seen from Hebrews 13:4 that the marriage bed is "undefiled," which indicates that sex is legitimate, holy and most pleasurable in marriage. Sexual immorality is found only outside the marriage covenant, and it refers to either fornication (sex between an unmarried person and anyone else) or adultery (sex between someone who is married and someone other than their spouse). David covers the whole realm of sexual impurity when he names the evil woman (adulteress) and the strange woman (prostitute).

I want you to picture Solomon, who was probably ten or twelve years old, with his eyes bugging out and a lump in his throat because his dad is pulling no punches. David is saying, "Solomon, you can experience sex God's way, or you can experience sex the world's way, which is backed by Satan.

"If you choose the world's way, you will not know how

to resist the prostitute or the adulteress. They are both roadblocks on the path to the woman God has for you. These women can destroy your capacity to love the right one."

The Strange Woman

The first thing we are told about the strange woman, the prostitute, is that she flatters with her words. This woman (or man) is a master when it comes to saying exactly what you want to hear.

> For the lips of a strange woman drop as an honeycomb, and her mouth is smoother than oil: But her end is bitter as wormwood, sharp as a two-edged sword (Proverbs 5:3-4).

There is a big difference between flattery and praise. Flattery tries to get something out of you; praise tries to put something into you. Flattery has an evil motivation behind it. It finds something good about you and uses it to take something from you. But praise wants to build you up and does not care whether you give anything in return.

The strange woman tells you that you are the best-looking thing she has ever seen in her life, and she gives you a false sense of worth through her deception. You can see why the prostitute is so despicable as she strokes you with her words and bats her eyelashes at you. She knows what to say at the right time to seduce you and take you with her — only to get something from you.

If you fall for this professional flattery, then the Scripture says "her mouth is smoother than oil" — boy, can she kiss! — but her end is as bitter as wormwood.

Wormwood is a wild plant from which a drug was made. At first when you chewed on it, it tasted sweet and made you feel great. But as the drug wore off it produced headaches and depression. If taken often enough, it could eventually destroy the mind.

Just like the powerful drug wormwood, the prostitute will give you a short time of sexual pleasure, but after the excitement comes a terrible bite. In the end, if you do not turn from her, the strange woman will use you until your very body and soul are destroyed. Wormwood tears away at the mind and eventually can kill the body. The prostitute does the same.

> Her feet go down to death; her steps take hold on hell (Proverbs 5:5).

In the ancient world, the feet were the main part of the body used by a woman to seduce a man, because very little of the body was exposed. Prostitutes attached small bells to their feet or put jewelry on them. They practiced small, seductive steps to catch a man's attention.

What this verse is literally saying is that the strange woman's seductive feet lead to death, and her steps run toward the grave.

> Lest thou shouldest ponder the path of life, her ways are moveable, that thou canst not know them (Proverbs 5:6).

David goes on to say, "Son, before you get involved with anyone like this, stand back and ponder it — think about it a minute. Her ways are moveable. She's shifty and manipulative, and you can never get her to commit to anything. She will tell you anything you want to hear in order to get your money. She tells you that you are the best lover and the most handsome guy she has ever seen. But if you hang around long enough, you'll hear her give the very same line to every other man she meets.

"The next day you may try to call her and find that her

phone has been disconnected, or she has moved. You go out to find her, but no one knows where she's gone. Then one day you run into her on the street or in the lobby of a hotel, and she's with another man, whispering seductively into his ear. When you go up to her, she won't even remember your name. Her ways are moveable, born out of the confusion and instability of her life, and you can never understand her."

> Hear me now therefore, O ye children, and depart not from the words of my mouth. Remove thy way far from her, and come not nigh the door of her house (Proverbs 5:7-8).

Trouble with the strange woman begins with curiosity. She will use curiosity to pull you into her bedroom! That is why David says to Solomon, "Don't even go near her. Be like your ancestor Joseph who didn't even stop to get his coat, but just ran out of the house when his master's wife tried to seduce him." When confronted by temptation, run from it! First Corinthians 6:18 says to flee fornication.

One of the lies that pressures young men to spend the night with a prostitute or a girl with a cheap reputation is that they need to gain sexual experience so they'll "know what they're doing" on their wedding night.

Apart from the fact that this goes against the clear teaching of Scripture to flee fornication, this lie contains another problem: If the relationship with your mate is established between your souls, then your mate is not going to want you to be experienced in sex with anyone but them. Your spouse wants to learn with you, and you will want to learn with them.

It is extremely unfortunate that most youth today give in to this kind of pressure and have sex before marriage. They are being cheated out of this intimate adventure which God designed to be one of the greatest pleasures of marriage.

Just How Strange Is the Strange Woman?

Many other passages of Scripture describe the strange woman. One of them is found in Proverbs 2:16-19:

> To deliver thee from the strange woman, even from the stranger which flattereth with her words; which forsaketh the guide of her youth, and forgetteth the covenant of her God. For her house inclineth unto death, and her paths unto the dead. None that go unto her return again, neither take they hold of the paths of life.

Again we are told that the strange woman is good with words; she is a flatterer. But then verse 17 tells us *why* she is what she is: She has turned away from "the guide of her youth" and has forgotten the covenant, or the words, of God. First of all, she has rebelled against the teaching of her parents, the guardians of her youth. After she rejected parental authority, it was very easy to reject God's authority also. When faced with the choice, she went her own way.

Many prostitutes, male and female, have grown up in the church. Some of them are even born again and know the Word of God. How do you think the Christian boy or girl can be so easily seduced? Prostitutes know what to say!

"Gee, I don't know why I kissed you. I guess I was just overwhelmed! I've never met anyone like you before."

"Well, wait just a minute. I'm a Christian and — "

"You are? So am I! This must be God! The Lord has brought us together to learn about love. After all, God is love."

"Yeah! This must be God."

And the foolish young believer is swept into fornication before they realize what is happening.

Many Christians laugh when I teach this, but they would sober up very fast if they listened to a few counseling sessions. People come to me with the most incredible stories. "My wife just wasn't satisfying me in bed, so God gave me a new secretary. Not only can she type ninety words a minute, but she satisfies me sexually. All she wants from me is a physical relationship — no strings attached — so I can go home and be much nicer to my wife. Isn't God good?"

I said to one man, "Aren't you special! Just for you and your particular problems, God broke His own Word, turned against His commandments and became a liar." In reality, these believers are coming to me to seek approval for their sin. They know deep down in their hearts that what they are doing is wrong.

The Third Man

Proverbs 7 offers a description of the believer who is "void of understanding." This is someone who has heard the truth but does not heed it — a hearer but not a doer.

If you look closely, you will see there are three people involved in this situation: the boy, the prostitute and the Lord Jesus Christ. David is making one more point to young Solomon: *Everything* you do is seen by the Lord. Nothing is done in secret.

> For at the window of my house I looked through my casement, and beheld among the simple ones, I discerned among the youths, a young man void of understanding, passing through the street near her corner; and he went the way to her house, in the twilight, in the evening, in the black and dark night: And, behold, there met him a woman with the attire of a harlot, and subtile of heart (Proverbs 7:6-10).

Here we have a curious young man who is deliberately

55

sneaking out in the dark to hang out near a known prostitute's house. Jesus is the one looking out of His window to observe it all.

> For the ways of man are before the eyes of the Lord, and he pondereth all his goings (Proverbs 5:21).

> Neither is there any creature that is not manifest in his sight: but all things are naked and opened unto the eyes of him with whom we have to do (Hebrews 4:13).

Your parents, your friends and your pastor may never know, but Jesus sees everything!

If this boy had understood and obeyed the instruction of his parents, he would not be where he is. But he believes that his parents are the ignorant ones. They just don't want him to have any fun, so he's decided to go over and take a look.

In verse 8, it says he was "passing through the street near her corner" but the word translated "passing" means "sauntering." When you're "passing," you're walking from one place to another; when you're "sauntering," you are bored and looking for trouble.

One of the most important things you can teach your children is how to handle restlessness and boredom. Tell them there are going to be times when they will have nothing to do and feel agitated. Their flesh is enticing them to sin, but their spirit is calling them to get into God's Word. These restless times are what we should all come to recognize as special times the Lord wants to spend with us.

Then, instead of running to mischief in frustration and boredom, we will turn to Scripture — study the words used, pray over them and meditate on them, listen to a tape or read a good book — and become stronger in the Lord.

But the boy who is sauntering through the streets is

thinking only of his own curiosity and selfish interests. He has given in to the agitations of his flesh. By the time the harlot approaches him, he has placed himself in a position to be deceived and hurt.

> So she caught him, and kissed him, and with an impudent face said unto him, I have peace offerings with me; this day have I payed my vows. Therefore came I forth to meet thee, diligently to seek thy face, and I have found thee (Proverbs 7:13-15).

It says in verse 13 that "she caught him." How did she catch him? She caught him with her words. Remember that flattery is the name of her game. Once he had fallen for her line, she kissed him. This is when he must have panicked and said, "I can't do this. I'm a Christian."

How do we know he said this? Because the next thing she says is that she has made peace offerings and paid her vows. She's literally saying, "That's great! I'm a Christian, too." She knows the language of believers either because she herself was raised in the church or because she has bedded down with many believers. She knows just what to say and how to say it.

She goes on to tell him how she came out to meet him — their coming together was God-arranged! In the next verses she describes how she has prepared herself for him, the special one God has sent to her to teach the ways of love.

> I have decked my bed with coverings of tapestry, with carved works, with fine linen of Egypt. I have perfumed my bed with myrrh, aloes, and cinnamon. Come, let us take our fill of love until the morning: let us solace ourselves with loves (Proverbs 7:16-18).

She is telling him that she is going to turn him into a first-class lover. He will be fully prepared when he gets married later. Notice that in verse 18 she says, "Let us solace ourselves with loves." In the Hebrew this literally means "to quench the thirst of." She knows she will quench his thirst but never satisfy it. Her intention is to hook him so he will come back for more.

> With her much fair speech she caused him to yield, with the flattering of her lips she forced him. He goeth after her straightway, as an ox goeth to the slaughter, or as a fool to the correction of the stocks; till a dart strike through his liver; as a bird hasteth to the snare, and knoweth not that it is for his life (Proverbs 7:21-23).

This kid swallowed her line about being a Christian and their meeting being arranged by God, and he went after her "straightway," or immediately. He is like a dumb animal being led to slaughter. If you've ever seen cows led to slaughter, they are not afraid or cautious in the least. They just follow along and stand there watching while the knife is raised. They don't know what is going on until it is too late.

The dart that strikes symbolizes the guilt that overwhelms later. It hits in the liver, which represents the deepest feelings and emotions. This guilt is so overwhelming that you will be an emotional wreck! It will strike deep inside of you and do tremendous damage to your life, yet no one may know but you and Jesus, the third Person who sees every thought and every move.

Stolen Waters

A foolish woman is clamorous: she is simple, and knoweth nothing. For she sitteth at the door of

> her house, on a seat in the high places of the city,
> to call passengers who go right on their ways:
> Whoso is simple, let him turn in hither: and as for
> him that wanteth understanding, she saith to him,
> Stolen waters are sweet, and bread eaten in se-
> cret is pleasant. But he knoweth not that the dead
> are there; and that her guests are in the depths of
> hell (Proverbs 9:13-18).

Here we read another passage about the strange woman, describing her as foolish and clamorous. She may appear to have a sweet and innocent facade, but her true nature is to be loud and noisy. She has been in rebellion toward the guardians of her youth and toward God Himself. This is evident by her attitude, her words and her loud voice.

She puts on a streetwise act as if she knows everything, but in fact she knows nothing. She is foolish. The Word of God says that the fear of the Lord is the beginning of knowledge (Proverbs 1:7), and she has rejected the Lord. It doesn't matter if you have a Ph.D. after your name; if you don't fear the Lord, you haven't even begun in wisdom.

Proverbs 9:14-15 tell us this woman is extremely restless and rarely stays at home. She has to be around other people and cannot be still and quiet. If God's will is not first in your life, you will become like the strange woman described here: sitting at your door, tapping your foot and waiting for the next thrill to come along.

Who is attracted to the strange woman? "Whoso is sim-ple...that wanteth understanding (v. 16)." Without under-standing of scriptural truths, the foolish person will be taken in by the false "wisdom" of the prostitute. She tells him, "Stolen waters are sweet, and bread eaten in secret is pleasant."

The word *waters* refers to the sex act. (We will look more closely at this in the next chapter.) The "waters" of the woman are intended to be sexual refreshment to her husband. "Stolen waters" are waters that do not belong to a man. This foolish woman is preaching that they are sweet. But remember that God said the waters will turn bitter, like wormwood.

She goes on to say that "bread eaten in secret is pleasant," which means that sinning behind closed doors is exciting and mysterious. It carries with it an exhilaration, a temporary high.

Both of these statements are true in that sin is exciting and pleasant for a season (Hebrews 11:25). Many people find it easy to justify their sin and even to deny the scriptural values with which they were raised because nothing bad happens to them at first. They are having the time of their lives and never felt better. "See, I've been living with my boyfriend for three months now. God hasn't struck me dead!"

> Be not deceived; God is not mocked: for whatsoever a man soweth, that shall he also reap. For he that soweth to his flesh shall of the flesh reap corruption; but he that soweth to the Spirit shall of the Spirit reap life everlasting (Galatians 6:7-8).

Eventually, if you don't repent and turn from it, your sin will bring destruction to your life. The Holy Spirit tells us that "the wages of sin is death" (Romans 6:23), which is also what David told Solomon in Proverbs 9:18: "the dead are there; and...her guests are in the depths of hell."

> Bread of deceit is sweet to a man; but afterwards his mouth shall be filled with gravel (Proverbs 20:17).

"Bread of deceit" is the same as "bread eaten in secret." What turns the pleasant bread into gravel? Guilt and condemnation, which, if not dealt with scripturally

(1 John 1:9), will transform a believer's life into a living hell on earth.

The Wages of Sin

Let's go back again to Proverbs 5 and take a good look at the consequences of a life of pursuing strange women (or men).

> Lest thou give thine honour unto others, and thy years unto the cruel: Lest strangers be filled with thy wealth; and thy labours be in the house of a stranger (Proverbs 5:9-10).

The Hebrew word for "honour" in verse 9 actually means "sexual strength." The honor of the man is his sexual strength, which he imparts to his wife in their marriage. As she is pleased and fulfilled in their lovemaking, she returns that honor back to her husband. The wife is the reflected honor and glory of her husband (1 Corinthians 11:7).

David is admonishing Solomon not to give his honor and glory to those who will never reflect it back to him, who will only be cruel and heartless when the seduction is over. "You will give them your sexual strength, and they will keep your 'labors' — your paycheck. You will give and give, but nothing will come back to refresh you and renew your strength. Eventually you will run out of money and strength and be totally empty."

> And thou mourn at the last, when thy flesh and thy body are consumed, and say, How have I hated instruction, and my heart despised reproof; and have not obeyed the voice of my teachers, nor inclined mine ear to them that instructed me! (Proverbs 5:11-13).

Verse 11 says you will "mourn" at the last, but the literal translation is "groan or howl." "Thy flesh" and "thy body" in this context refer to the sexual organs. You will groan at the last because your body will be so ravaged by disease that your sexual organs will no longer respond. Your final days will consist of groaning, torment, pain and impotence. Not a very macho end for the male stud! (Nor a very glamorous end for the female seductress.)

Why does the macho man wind up being an impotent wreck? Because he "hated instruction," "despised reproof" and rejected and disobeyed his parents and teachers, who instructed him in the ways of God. Again, David says to Solomon, "Don't just *hear* the instruction of God, but *live* it."

> For by means of a whorish woman a man is brought to a piece of bread (Proverbs 6:26).

What this verse really says is, "The price of a whore is about one loaf of bread." The prostitute is just trying to make enough money to eat that day — one loaf of bread. She will use her body and any deceptive means it takes to get it from you. You mean nothing more to her than her meals for the day.

The obvious and immediate result of having sex with a prostitute is that your money is taken. But the long-term effects of bedding down with prostitutes are "sharp as a two-edged sword" (Proverbs 5:4). Not only is your money taken for a temporary high, but your body is subjected to sexual diseases, and your mind is plagued with confusion and guilt.

> I was almost in all evil in the midst of the congregation and assembly (Proverbs 5:14).

Final humiliation comes when your sin is made known.

If you are a believer, it will be known in the church first. It is incredible to me that a believer who is living in fornication or adultery thinks nobody is aware of what's happening. You are usually the last to discover that everyone knows.

This verse goes on to tell us that not only has his evil been exposed in the church (congregation), but his good reputation has been destroyed among society at large (assembly). When he becomes painfully aware that his secret life is publicly exposed, it is one of the hardest things for him to face.

The Evil Woman

Getting involved with an evil woman, or adulteress, can be even more disastrous than becoming entangled in fornication with strange women. Adultery is not a one-night stand but an affair that goes on week after week and month after month. It slowly drains the life out of you.

You are not designed spiritually, mentally, emotionally or physically to function with and commit yourself to more than one person. When you enter into adultery, you begin the process of destroying your ability to love. God did not design you to give yourself to everybody. He created you to be joined together with one person.

A double minded man is unstable in all his ways
(James 1:8).

When your heart and mind are torn between the sacred and holy covenant with your spouse and the false and fleeting exhilaration of a "new love," you are double minded. Instability and confusion will reign in all areas of your life until you repent and turn from your sin altogether.

The adulteress is even more wicked than the strange woman. Where the prostitute just wants your money, the adulteress wants your very life.

And the adulteress will hunt for the precious life (Proverbs 6:26).

The adulteress can have sex with her husband, so it isn't just sex that she wants from you. She has possessions with her husband, so it isn't your money that she wants. She wants to *possess your very soul.* It's often a game of power and control with her.

In the following verses of Scripture, David tells Solomon just how foolish it is to get involved in adultery.

> So he that goeth in to his neighbour's wife; whosoever toucheth her shall not be innocent. Men do not despise a thief, if he steal to satisfy his soul when he is hungry; but if he be found, he shall restore sevenfold; he shall give all the substance of his house.
>
> But whoso committeth adultery with a woman lacketh understanding: he that doeth it destroyeth his own soul. A wound and dishonour shall he get; and his reproach shall not be wiped away. For jealousy is the rage of a man: therefore he will not spare in the day of vengeance. He will not regard any ransom; neither will he rest content, though thou givest many gifts (Proverbs 6:29-35).

"A wound and dishonour shall he get." The results of giving in to the evil woman (adultery) are similar to those of falling for the strange woman (fornication). The "wound" represents the physical destruction that occurs. But dishonor happens in the soul and refers to an additional moral sting that comes from adultery. *You have stolen something that can never be paid back.*

What happens to a thief when he's caught stealing bread? Verse 31 says he will restore back sevenfold what he has stolen. But the thief who takes another man's wife "lacks understanding," which is the King James way of saying that he's just plain stupid. Why? Because he's not only destroying his own soul, but there is no way he can ever pay back what he has stolen.

How do you pay someone back for stealing a wife or husband? There is not enough money, nor can anything be said or done that will restore to a husband or wife what has been lost through the adultery of a spouse. "He will not regard any ransom; neither will he rest content, though thou givest many gifts."

Adultery is a unique crime in that it turns a pure relationship between a husband and a wife into a tainted one. The only way the marriage can be restored is if the husband and wife recommit their lives to God and to one another. They have to agree to forgive each other and allow God supernaturally to heal all the wounds and damage this grievous sin has caused.

> I made a covenant with my eyes: why then should I think upon a maid? (Job 31:1).

In this verse we see two important things. First, the covenant between a husband and wife is made in the soul. Throughout the Word of God the eyes refer to the mind and the soul (Matthew 6:22; Ephesians 1:18).

Because the covenant is in the soul, the sin occurs in the soul.

Second, we see more precisely where adultery begins — in the thoughts of the soul: "Why then should I *think* upon a maid?" Jesus said that if you look (meditate) upon a woman to lust after her, you've already committed adultery with her in your heart (Matthew 5:28).

Long before the sin ever manifests in the deed, it is first meditated upon in the mind.

The physical act of adultery is a direct result of breaking

covenant with your spouse in the mind. As you fantasize about someone else, dishonor enters the soul, and you open yourself up to the actual act of adultery. That act will spoil your reputation and destroy your good name.

Job shows just how ridiculous it is to try to justify yourself and clear your name after adultery is committed.

> If mine heart have been deceived by a woman, or if I have laid wait at my neighbour's door; then let my wife grind unto another, and let others bow down upon her (Job 31:9-10).

How do you pay back what has been stolen by adultery? Give the wronged spouse your wife or husband?

> For this is an heinous crime; yea, it is an iniquity to be punished by the judges. For it is a fire that consumeth to destruction, and would root out all mine increase (Job 31:11-12).

As Job pointed out in this last verse of Scripture, adultery will not only dishonor your name, but it will also cut off your financial prosperity.

Not only is your testimony for the Lord destroyed, but your finances that support the preaching of the gospel are cut off. We see this principle at work even in the world. A wealthy man commits adultery and loses his fortune in the process.

Deep in their hearts, no matter what their professed values, people cannot trust a man who is unfaithful to his wife or a woman who is unfaithful to her husband. They begin to wonder, "If he cheated on his spouse and lied to her, will he cheat me and lie to me also?" This is part of the destruction of the adulterer's soul which eventually brings destruction to his finances.

> And why wilt thou, my son, be ravished with a
> strange woman, and embrace the bosom of a
> stranger? For the ways of man are before the eyes of
> the Lord, and he pondereth [weighs in the bal-
> ance] all his goings. His own iniquities shall take
> the wicked himself, and he shall be holden with
> the cords [chains] of his sins (Proverbs 5:20-22).

The sex life of a man or woman is always known by the
Lord. According to verse 21, He weighs in the balances
(ponders) all of our actions. The Bible goes on to say we
will be held by the cords, or chains, of our sins.

Sexual and moral freedom abound within the boundaries
of marriage. Commitment brings liberty. If a man gets
strapped to an evil woman or a strange woman, he places
himself in chains of bondage. He may try to break free, but
it will take a supernatural miracle to accomplish it, because
those chains will jerk him back to his sin again and again.

Whenever you are tempted to commit adultery, you can
feel true love restraining you. That is not just your covenant
with your mate; it is your covenant with God. Only a strong
love for your mate and a strong love for God will give you
the power to resist the temptation of sexual sin.

There is one more interesting facet of adultery that the
Bible brings out.

> There be three things which are too wonderful
> for me, yea, four which I know not: The way of
> an eagle in the air; the way of a serpent upon a
> rock; the way of a ship in the midst of the sea;
> and the way of a man with a maid. Such is the
> way of an adulterous woman; she eateth, and
> wipeth her mouth, and saith, I have done no
> wickedness (Proverbs 30:18-20).

What do all these things have in common? *None of them*

leaves a trail. There is no proof the eagle flew through the air over your head; there is no proof the serpent slithered across the rock at your feet; there is no proof the ship passed a certain way on the sea; and there is no proof that a man and woman had sexual relations.

This is the attitude of the adulterous woman. She has sexual relations with you, wipes her mouth and says, "It never happened. You can't prove anything. I haven't done anything wrong." She leaves no trail, and it is as though your relationship with her never happened.

When your sin eventually comes to light, the Bible says you will be exposed in the midst of the congregation and disgraced publicly. You will point to the one who seduced you and plead, saying that you were ensnared by this evil woman, but she will deny everything, and there will be no trail. A momentary thrill has robbed you of part of your life.

A Wise King's Foolish Choice

No one understood the consequences of sexual immorality better than Solomon. Yet, in 1 Kings 11, we discover something that is both astounding and grievous: Solomon did not heed his father's advice.

> But king Solomon loved many strange women, together with the daughter of Pharaoh, women of the Moabites, Ammonites, Edomites, Zidonians, and Hittites; of the nations concerning which the Lord said unto the children of Israel, Ye shall not go in to them, neither shall they come in unto you: for surely they will turn away your heart after their gods: Solomon clave unto these in love.
>
> And he had seven hundred wives, princesses, and three hundred concubines: and his wives turned away his heart (vv. 1-3).

Solomon loved many strange women despite his father's godly counsel. Notice that verse 3 refers to his wives as "princesses." What this means is that the women he married were daughters of the kings in their own countries. Solomon married these princesses to "buy" peace with the surrounding countries.

Why does the Bible refer to these princesses as "strange women"? Their nations were enemies of God as well as of Israel, and their religions centered around sex. These princesses, who were priestesses in their temples, were nothing more than aristocratic prostitutes.

It also says in verse 3 that Solomon had three hundred concubines, or royal mistresses. A mistress is someone with whom he would have sex, but to whom he was not married. When it came to sexual immorality, Solomon did it all.

The wisest king the world has ever known made a foolish choice in his life, and the results were tragic. By choosing his selfish desires over the instruction of his parents, he did incredible damage to himself, his family and the entire nation of Israel.

One of the greatest deceptions surrounding sexual sin is that it doesn't harm anyone but you and your partner.

First Kings 11:3 says, "His wives turned away his heart." When you engage in sexual immorality, you enter into confusion and every evil work because you have no fellowship with the Lord. Just consider the mathematics of Solomon's sex life, and you will understand his level of confusion. If he had sex with a different wife or concubine every night, it would take him almost three years to go through them all!

Living in such chaos, Solomon tore down all the altars to the Lord and built altars to the idols of his wives in their places. The seeds of idolatry that he planted in Israel kept the people in bondage to false gods for a period of time spanning the reign of eight kings after him, including the most despicable, Ahab, and his wife, Jezebel.

Solomon listened to his father's teaching so well that he managed to write it all down in the Book of Proverbs, but he reached a point in his life when he chose not to follow his father's wisdom. The Book of Ecclesiastes, also written by Solomon, points out the futility and worthlessness he experienced as he lived according to his own carnal desires. His entire perspective is summed up in the first two verses of the book:

> The words of the Preacher, the son of David, king in Jerusalem. Vanity of vanities, saith the Preacher, vanity of vanities; all is vanity (Ecclesiastes 1:1-2).

The Hebrew word translated "vanity" means empty and dead, separated from the life of God. A life of sexual sin is an empty life. Solomon not only learned that from his father, but unfortunately he decided to experience it for himself. Furthermore, when we get to another book in the Bible which Solomon wrote, Song of Solomon, we will see how he came to long for the one-flesh relationship found only in marriage to one person.

Ecclesiastes 12 suggests that later in his life Solomon turned back to the Lord. But during his years of apostasy he brought misery to himself and those around him.

A Word of Hope to Those Who Have Fallen

Marriage was designed by God to build you up, but adultery and fornication tear you down, little by little. I will not mince words here: Sexual immorality is sin, and it will destroy your life. But if you have fallen in this area, you can be changed, healed and restored.

Jesus said He did not come into this world to condemn us but to save us and set us free (see John 3:17). First John 1:9 says, "If we confess our sins, he is faithful and just to forgive us our sins, and to cleanse us from all unrighteousness." I have seen God, time after time, take marriages that were on the rocks and transform them into something phenomenal.

When a husband and wife make the commitment to love each other and allow the Holy Spirit to change them, there is no limit to the blessings God will bestow on their marriage. I have seen some marriages so altered that anyone who didn't know the two people before would never guess they ever had a problem.

And to the single person who has experienced sexual immorality — even homosexuality, lesbianism and sexual abuse — I say this: God can take your life and totally transform it if you will seek the help you need and dedicate yourself to the power of the Word and prayer.

Freedom from sexual sin doesn't come easily. It takes a completely dedicated heart to break away and stay free. You must study God's way of thinking about sex, relationships and marriage — and you must pray. Find a godly pastor and attend church faithfully to hear what God is saying to you.

Something else is vitally important: Seek fellowship with godly men and women in and out of church, cutting off all relationships which jeopardize your spiritual well-being. In most cases you will need a good Christian counselor to help you tear down the strongholds that led you into sexual immorality. They will help you build godly strongholds in their place.

Some people say that a bird with a broken wing will never fly as high again. This may be true in nature, but it does not apply to the grace of God. The beauty and miracle of knowing Jesus Christ as Lord and Savior is that even after you have made a mess of your life, if you repent and receive forgiveness, and if you embrace His Word and commit yourself to the Spirit's leading, you can fly higher than you've ever flown before!

71

No one knew this truth better than David. He committed adultery with Bathsheba, killed her husband when he learned she was pregnant with his child and married her in an attempt to cover his sin. Though they started out on very shaky ground, David and Bathsheba turned to God and worked together to build one of the best marriages in Israel's history.

In the last days of his life, David wrote:

> Bless the Lord, O my soul, and forget not all his benefits: Who forgiveth all thine iniquities; who healeth all thy diseases; who redeemeth thy life from destruction; who crowneth thee with lovingkindness and tender mercies; who satisfieth thy mouth with good things; so that thy youth is renewed like the eagle's (Psalms 103:2-5). ❧

THREE

A Famous Father Speaks Frankly to His Son About Sex Part Two: The Righteous Way

Most public schools today teach children that sex in any form is acceptable and that sexual experimentation at a young age is normal and healthy. They are warned about AIDS and other sexually transmitted diseases and are encouraged to practice "safe sex," which means using a condom. Students are also cautioned that, without some form of birth control, a girl could become pregnant and have to make a choice between having a baby or aborting it.

The practical consequences of their actions are mentioned, but if a moral standard is given to our youth, it is not a biblical one. In terms of morality, young people are led to believe they are their own standard. Relying on their parents' values is an option, but it is not encouraged. They must decide what is right for them.

As times change and world values change, so do the moral standards of the society in which we live. God, on the other hand, has laid down a standard that doesn't vary with circumstances and that can be relied upon totally. He does not tell us to flee fornication and adultery because He wants us to live miserable lives. He is not trying to keep us from having fun. He's trying to keep us from ending up like the macho man described in Proverbs 5 — lying on his bed groaning in impotence and tormented by disease.

God has designed sex to be practiced within the boundaries of marriage so it can be one of the most fantastic experiences of our lives. Instead of coming to the end of our lives early, emaciated by sexual immorality, we can live long, satisfying and prosperous lives.

God does not place in us a passion to be one with someone of the opposite sex and then tell us it is wrong or perverted. He laid a framework and set down guidelines for us in which the purity and holiness of sex can be preserved and protected. In this way it can remain one of life's greatest blessings.

Waters of Refreshing

We have heard David tell Solomon many times to save himself for his mate, to preserve himself until the day he is married to the one God has for him. Instead, Solomon rejected his father's wisdom, married many strange women and had many mistresses.

In the following verses of Scripture Solomon tells us what he missed by turning away from God's plan and instead going his own way. This is advice from his father that he did not heed.

> Drink waters out of thine own cistern, and running waters out of thine own well. Let thy fountains be dispersed abroad, and rivers of waters in the streets. Let them be only thine own, and not strangers' with thee. Let thy fountain be blessed: and rejoice with the wife of thy youth. Let her be as the loving hind and pleasant roe; let her breasts satisfy thee at all times; and be thou ravished always with her love (Proverbs 5:15-19).

The cistern and the well are scriptural analogies for the woman, and the fountain represents the man. Obviously, they all contain water. Water is a symbol for the gift of sexual pleasure which God intended to be given to both spouses. The water in the well belongs to the wife, but it is intended to satisfy the sexual thirst of her husband. Likewise, the water in the fountain belongs to the husband, but it is intended to satisfy the sexual thirst of his wife.

Water is a symbol for two other things in Scripture. First, it symbolizes the new birth or salvation.

> Ho, every one that thirsteth, come ye to the waters, and he that hath no money; come ye, buy, and eat (Isaiah 55:1).

Remember the day when you were thirsty for truth, for the presence and power of God, and Jesus brought you the "living water"? He told the woman at the well that she could drink the natural water of the well and be thirsty again, but He could give her a well that "shall be in [you] a well of water springing up into everlasting life" (John 4:14).

The new birth satisfies the thirst for God on the inside of you, but every day there is still a thirst for more of God.

This brings us to the second thing water symbolizes in Scripture.

> That he might sanctify and cleanse it with the washing of water by the word (Ephesians 5:26).

God provides fresh water for us every day in His Word. In the same way we physically need food and water daily, we spiritually hunger and thirst after righteousness every day. Jesus said: "Man shall not live by bread alone, but by every word of God" (Luke 4:4).

God provided a well of eternal life inside us when we were born again, but He also provided a well of Scripture from which we can draw refreshment and receive cleansing every day.

Physically, water quenches the thirst; it refreshes, cleans and strengthens the body. In spiritual terms, water is used to symbolize the new birth and the Word of God, which is our spiritual food and refreshment. In the same way, having sex with your wife or husband is designed by God to satisfy your sexual desire, to refresh you and to strengthen your relationship on a continual basis.

There is a third aspect of water that is most important: It is a grace gift. Grace means you can't work for it, earn it or deserve it. Water is given by God freely to everyone (Matthew 5:45). It is a natural symbol representing God's spiritual blessings and unconditional love.

You couldn't buy your salvation, and you certainly don't deserve to be saved. Yet, "while we were yet sinners, Christ died for us" (Romans 5:8). The new birth was a gift of the grace of God. It is the same with the gift of God's Word. He gave it to you because He freely and lovingly chose to give it.

A husband and wife are grace gifts to one another. Eve was God's grace gift to Adam; Adam was God's grace gift to Eve. This means that your mate is as much a gift of God's unconditional love to you as salvation and His Word are. Therefore, you should not misuse or abuse this special person. Your mate should be as sacred to you as the miracle of being in Christ or having His exceeding great and precious promises available to you daily.

Sexual strength is a gift of grace, too. As it was graciously given to you, you should graciously reserve it for your mate. A gift can be abused, pearls can be cast before swine, and sex can be cheapened through promiscuity. Save your waters of refreshing for the right one.

God gave you the gift of sex, but it has someone else's name on it!

The Power of Virginity

There is a difference between a cistern and a well. A cistern is covered and a well is not. Throughout the Word of God a cistern indicates a virgin, a well that is sealed until its owner comes to uncover it and partake of it. Once the cistern has been uncovered, the owner has his own personal well to satisfy his thirst. This is the wife's relationship to her husband.

"Drinking out of your own cistern" is an idiom used throughout the Scriptures which means to have sex with your mate. There is an example of this in 2 Kings 18 in which Sennacherib and his army were about to attack Jerusalem. He sent one of his men, Rabshakeh, to speak to Jerusalem before the attack.

Rabshakeh walked up to the city gates and announced to the people that if they insisted on fighting, they would all be killed. However, if they would surrender, they could "drink...every one the waters of his cistern" (2 Kings 18:31). In other words, husbands could keep their wives.

When a virgin opens herself up and allows her husband to take the seal off her cistern, she has a pure well of water to refresh and replenish him. She can't give too much love to him, because every time she gives to him, he gives back even more to her.

If a woman indiscriminately lets every man partake of her water, or sexual favors, her water will become impure and eventually diseased. Soon the waters will be gone from her well. She can only give so many times to those who have no right to it, because only her husband can replenish her.

A man's sex drive is called a fountain in Proverbs 5:16. A virgin husband refreshes and replenishes his wife with the pure water of his fountain. When a woman meets her husband, he has the God-given capacity as her fountain to replace and replenish the water she provides for him. However, if a man brings his fountain to any well, his water will become impure and eventually diseased as well. He too will soon run dry.

It is a known fact that purity brings strength and pleasure. Every goldsmith and silversmith knows this. The purer the metal, the stronger it is, and the more pleasant it is to behold. Likewise in marriage, the purer the relationship, the stronger and more pleasurable it will be. Virginity before marriage and fidelity after marriage ensure both the health and pleasure of sex, which becomes better even into old age.

Only your mate can provide pure refreshment and return the physical love you give them.

The Fountain Meets the Well — Honeymoon Blues

The difference between a well and a fountain is that a well is calm, but a fountain is water under pressure. A man's sex drive is more predominant than a woman's. To put it bluntly, a man is always ready, but a woman needs to be stirred up! And, husbands, holding back the pressure to give the water time to stir will always pay great dividends.

I've talked to wives in counseling sessions who said, "I

just didn't understand what a man was like when I got married. The slightest thing turns him on! He's ready to make love at the drop of a hat, and it drives me crazy!" When I tell them God made men that way, that this is not an evil thing, they are not always thrilled. But a wife needs to understand the sexual pressure within her husband; she needs to realize that one of his strongest desires is to make love to her.

I think a tragedy in our society is the glorification of the honeymoon. It is supposed to be one of the greatest times of marriage, but it is probably one of the worst. Newlyweds don't know what they are doing. The new bride doesn't understand her husband's aggressive nature in sex, and the bridegroom doesn't understand that his wife needs for him to take his time with her. Wise counsel and good books will help, but nothing can substitute for the experience they are about to get.

Have you ever seen a boy when he gets his first car? He's learned about driving from watching his father in his auto-matic-everything vehicle, but now the boy has a car of his own. He thinks it is the greatest thing in the world. Of course, it has a five-speed standard transmission, and he has never operated one before. But he is oblivious to his ignorance because he is so in love with his car.

Now, what happens the first time he gets in, turns the ignition and puts it in gear? He's not used to the clutch, he's not used to shifting gears, and he probably doesn't know that before he shifts into reverse he should shift into one of the other gears, or else it grinds. So he slowly moves out of the driveway, lurching and jumping.

Finally he gets it in gear, but then he releases the clutch too soon and doesn't give it enough gas. So he kills the engine and has to start over. He starts the engine again, but this time he decides he's going to hold down the clutch and give it lots of gas, then slowly release the clutch. He lays rubber all the way down the block. Thank

God the car is forgiving and can be restarted!

Until he learns how the car operates — where the clutch engages, how to shift gears smoothly and when to give it gas — he is going to have a bumpy ride. And this is just how the honeymoon is — you grind more gears and kill more engines than you've ever imagined in your life!

What happens when water under pressure, a fountain, is placed into a still well that has never been touched? Quite a disturbance! Many hurts and misconceptions occur as you get to know each other in this new, intimate way. Be patient and forgiving — and willing to restart your engine many times!

The world operates under the delusion that it is better for a man to be experienced sexually before marriage. Then he can be Mr. Wonderful on the honeymoon. Other than the fact that this goes against God's Word, there's one major problem: Every woman is different.

God has given one man for one woman, and only her husband — the man God has brought to her — is going to be able to satisfy her. She is not looking for a macho sex athlete or "Mr. Sexually Perfect." She is looking for a warm, caring man who will forgive his new wife for her mistakes as many times as she will forgive him.

Sexually, you may both be green. Neither one of you may know what you're doing. But you learn about each other, forgive one another, talk things out and try again and again until you learn how to please and respond to one another.

Again, if you have established a strong foundation of trust and understanding between yourselves, you will be able to forgive each other easily and try again. Then, as you love each other through it, you begin to flow together, and sex continues to get better through the years.

> Drink waters out of thine own cistern, and running waters out of thine own well (Proverbs 5:15).

This verse assures us that, after the wife is first stirred up, her waters will begin to flow. Once you uncover your cistern and drink waters from it, from that time on you will have more and more running, or flowing, waters in your well. Literally, the wife's desire for sex will increase, and her own sexual aggressiveness will develop. If you patiently love each other through the honeymoon, you will have wonderful times ahead of you!

Rejoice With the Wife of Your Youth

Water is designed to satisfy thirst, and God has ordained that the husband and wife satisfy their sexual thirst with the pure waters of his fountain and her well. With this analogy in mind, let's look at Proverbs 23:27.

> For a whore is a deep ditch; and a strange woman is a narrow pit.

(When was the last time you pulled that one out of your promise box?)

If you were thirsty and it had just rained outside, would you go to a ditch or a mud puddle and drink from it? I would think something was seriously wrong with you if you did. Yet that is exactly what you are doing when you go to a prostitute or someone other than your mate to satisfy the thirst of your sexual desire. In the end your thirst will not be quenched, and you can easily become sick or diseased.

In the ancient world there were many public wells, but cisterns were privately owned by individuals. Because many different people drank from the public wells, they became polluted and were often filled with disease. Sometimes whole cities moved because the open wells had gone bad.

Some of the greatest stories in the Bible revolve around a piece of property where God provided a cistern — a well of fresh water that was only for a certain person and his family. That is what marriage is like. You are the exclusive thirst quenchers for each other!

> Let thy fountains be dispersed abroad, and rivers of waters in the streets. Let them be only thine own, and not strangers' with thee (Proverbs 5:16-17).

This is an incorrect translation for verse 16, which really says, "Let *not* thy fountains be dispersed abroad." Do you know what happens to a fountain when it is dispersed? Not only does it run out of water, but it runs in little rivers down the streets. Men, if you disperse your fountain abroad, you are going to have little rivers running up and down the street!

How embarrassing to be strolling down the street with your wife and family and suddenly have another child, a "little river," run up to you saying, "Hi, Daddy!" The Bible exhorts you strongly to reserve your fountain for your wife alone. With all the metaphors, men, I don't want you to miss the point of this verse: The only woman who has access to your zipper is your wife!

> Let thy fountain be blessed: and rejoice with the wife of thy youth (Proverbs 5:18).

God's desire is for a man to be blessed sexually, and that happens when he rejoices with the wife of his youth. Here the Hebrew word translated "rejoice" means the same as rejoicing before the Lord: to be emotionally happy, ecstatic and to shout with joy. Instead of ending his days in impotence and groaning, he will be so in love with his wife that he will be shouting and rejoicing!

There has always been a teaching in the Body of Christ that God created sex only for the purpose of having children, but that is simply not true. When God told the husband to cleave to his wife and become one flesh with her, He didn't add, "in order to have children."

God ordained sex for pleasure and refreshment, and that is why it is compared to a well of water (the woman) being joined with a fountain (the man). As they draw from each other, they are also giving back to one another. Only a husband and wife can replenish each other. This is why, in a loving marriage relationship, romance and sex become better through the years. That's good reason to shout!

> Let her be as the loving hind and pleasant roe; let her breasts satisfy thee at all times; and be thou ravished always with her love (Proverbs 5:19).

The "hind" is referring to a doe or a female deer, and the "roe" is referring to a she-goat. The she-goat and the doe were greatly appreciated in the ancient world for their beautiful symmetry. Also, the word for "pleasant" means "grace," which is reminding us that the wife's body is a gift of grace to her husband.

Although this verse says the wife should satisfy her husband at all times, it does not mean that whenever he snaps his fingers, she should start marching to the bedroom. What this is saying is that she *alone* will satisfy her husband. Her husband is not to try to satisfy his sexual thirst with anyone else.

Another thing I want to point out to wives is just what the Scripture says: Your breasts are for your husband's pleasure — no one else's — and you are not to withhold them from him or be embarrassed by the fact that he enjoys them. God gave them to you for his pleasure, not just to breast-feed children. Like the sealed cistern, this part of your body should remain covered until you are married. But once your husband lifts the covering, your breasts and your body are for his enjoyment.

When the Bible says that Adam and Eve were naked but not ashamed (Genesis 2:25), the word *ashamed* means "embarrassed." They were not embarrassed about their naked bodies. They enjoyed looking at each other and touching each other and didn't think anything of it. After all, God does not turn His head when we take our clothes off. He knows what we look like, and it doesn't bother Him.

On the other hand, you are not to expose yourself to anyone but your spouse. It is so important for men and women to understand that dressing modestly brings honor to their marriage. Husbands and wives who wear clothing that exposes too much of their bodies to others are showing dissatisfaction with their mates and giving an open invitation to the public.

Drunk in Love

In marriage, our bodies are to give pleasure to one another, but Proverbs 5:19 is saying more than just, "Have a good time, kids!" It says we are to be ravished, or "intoxicated," when we make love to our mate. We are to be drunk in love with each other. I remind you this is God's idea of a good time!

If you have ever known an alcoholic, you know he cannot go too long without having a drink. More than that, during the times he is not drinking, he imagines what the next drink is going to be like. He is drunk many times mentally before he ever touches the bottle. Alcohol controls his thoughts and possesses his soul.

In the same way, there is nothing wrong with a husband fantasizing about making love to his wife. The devil perverts the purpose of the imagination by turning men and women's thoughts to sexual immorality, but here we have the Word of God telling the husband to be intoxicated or drunk with love for his wife. He can mentally make love to her many times before he hits the door after work that evening.

Or maybe he begins to think about her and imagine

what it will be like to be with her again, and he calls her and says, "Honey, I just wanted to hear your voice, and I can't wait to see you tonight."

When five o'clock rolls around, he runs out to his car like a madman and lays rubber all the way out of the parking lot. He stops to pick up her favorite flowers and peels off toward home. When she finally stands before him and gives him that welcome-home kiss, he's like a wino sniffing the cork. He knows he's going to get drunk tonight!

Love is not just sex, but sex is a powerful expression of love. An alcoholic drinks because alcohol controls his soul. He drinks as a manifestation of his being possessed by it. Marriage is not sex, but sex is an outward expression of a soul possessed with love for the husband or wife. The Bible warns against drunkenness on wine, but tells us there is no limit to being drunk with love for your mate!

Solomon's Folly

Solomon had the finest instructor in David, and we have seen that David pulled no punches when he talked to his son about sex and marriage. Solomon listened, and by the time he wrote the Proverbs, he was probably at the height of his reign as the wisest king Israel — and the world — has ever known.

The Word of God declares that Solomon was blessed with great wisdom because he did not seek after gold and silver, long life or fame. He sought after wisdom in order to rightly judge the Lord's people. Because his heart was right before the Lord, God gave him riches along with great wisdom. In terms of values and priorities, Solomon was "seeking first the kingdom of God, and His righteousness," and therefore all other things were given to him (Matthew 6:33).

As he followed the precepts of his father, there was a time when his wisdom was so staggering that kings, queens and people from all over the earth came to witness it for themselves. When the Queen of Sheba came to see him, she left breathless, saying, "Behold, the half was not told me" (1 Kings 10:7).

However, there was one thing Solomon did not do early in life, and that was to marry. Eventually he turned from his father's teachings and decided to search things out for himself. He tried to fill this void in his life by satisfying his own desires and curiosity instead of following the instructions of his parents and the plan of God.

Many people try to put God on a shelf and find fulfillment apart from Him, but this is impossible. We are made in God's image, and therefore only His Spirit and His Word can fulfill our lives.

God has ordained happiness for each day, but we have to follow His plan. In Solomon's own words, when you follow your own plan, there is nothing ahead but "vexation of spirit."

> I have seen all the works that are done under the sun; and, behold, all is vanity and vexation of spirit (Ecclesiastes 1:14).

The word *ecclesiastes* simply means "preacher," but *preacher* means more than a man who stands in a pulpit. He is the one who has the message for the hour. Solomon is the preacher with the message for both his hour and ours in the Book of Ecclesiastes.

Ecclesiastes is not the most pleasant book to read. In fact, reading it could leave you depressed. God made it part of His Word because He wanted us to hear from someone who plunged from the mountaintop to the deepest valley, someone who knew the wisdom of God's Word but turned away from it to go his own way. Consequently, he went from the height of success to the depths of despair. That man was the great King Solomon.

> I applied mine heart to know, and to search, and
> to seek out wisdom, and the reason of things,
> and to know the wickedness of folly, even of
> foolishness and madness (Ecclesiastes 7:25).

Solomon made a cold, calculated decision to find out for
himself what wickedness was really like. This is extremely
dangerous. Instead of accepting the truth of God's Word
and following the wisdom of his earthly father, Solomon
chose to experience wickedness for himself.

The Bible does not require proving by any man — it will
supernaturally reveal and prove itself to you. And it goes
without saying that if you trust God and His plan, then you
will be blessed. But if you go against Him and His Word,
your life will be filled with turmoil and pain. This is the
"folly" Solomon went after.

Solomon states that the folly he pursued included fool-
ishness and madness, which was wrapped up in sexual
promiscuity. Evidently Solomon had a tremendous sex
drive, but instead of looking forward to the time when God
would bring the right woman to him, he went after women.
He had a harem that put Egypt to shame.

> And I find more bitter than death the woman,
> whose heart is snares and nets, and her hands as
> bands: whoso pleaseth God shall escape from
> her; but the sinner shall be taken by her (Ecclesi-
> astes 7:26).

What was his conclusion after all was said and done? He
found the life of sexual promiscuity "more bitter than
death." And what was it that trapped him in this life of
sin? The heart of the woman, which is "snares and nets,
and her hands as bands." He pictures himself as a dumb
animal walking into the hunter's net.

Promiscuity was a trap. The strange and evil women's

hands were like chains that held him so there was no escape. The key to his escape, however, is given in this same verse: "Whoso pleaseth God shall escape from her."

The only remedy for the hold of immorality, the fantasies of pornography and the lust for sexual pleasure is total reliance on the delivering power of the Holy Spirit and God's promises. If you cling to His Word and Spirit, no chain of Satan can withstand the power of God (Luke 10:19).

Solomon saw that the only way out was by pleasing the Lord. We please the Lord and we are free when we abide in His Word and His Word abides in us (John 8:31-32). So if you are caught up in this "folly" of sexual sin, turn back to the Lord. It's never too late! Rely on His power. Read His Word, meditate on it and act on it, and you will surely escape and remain free.

Father Knows Best

> Behold, this have I found, saith the preacher, counting one by one, to find out the account: Which yet my soul seeketh, but I find not: one man among a thousand have I found; but a woman among all those have I not found (Ecclesiastes 7:27-28).

When Solomon says he counted one by one, it means he had one woman at a time. If he had one woman a day, it took him over three years to conclude that he had not found the woman God wanted for him. Do you know why he had not found her after experiencing more than a thousand women?

You don't find a mate by shopping around and sampling the merchandise. As you please God and wait on Him, He will bring you and your mate together. Your spirit will know by the Spirit of God that he or she is the right one.

Adam did the will of God, and on the right day, Eve was brought to him.

I've talked with so many believers who have found their mates by pleasing God. Almost all of them say, "When I first met them, something inside me said they were the one. Later, as we dated and got to know one another, we didn't think so at times! But through it all, as we worked out our problems and learned to communicate with each other, that 'knowing' became stronger and stronger. Soon God confirmed that this was the one He had sent."

Solomon shopped for a wife like a man would shop for a new suit. But marriage is a supernatural arrangement, and your husband or wife is a grace gift given by God. You do not need to go from place to place looking at all the available men or women, trying to decide who would be best for you. God knows who will fit you best. And He also knows how and when to bring you together.

One thing is painfully clear from verse 28. After satisfying his lust for women, Solomon's soul was still frustrated and unfulfilled. He found out the hard way that love does not begin from the outside and work its way in.

Love begins on the inside as two hearts recognize the hand of God on their lives.

> "Which yet my soul seeketh, but I find not" (Ecclesiastes 7:28).

The sad part is that Solomon stayed in sexual perversion so long, by the time he reached rock bottom and turned back to the Lord, it was too late to find the right woman. He died without experiencing "one flesh" himself. By turning from the plan of God and going off on his own to find happiness, he missed the very happiness he craved.

Again we come back to the principle of grace. Your husband or wife is a gift of grace that you cannot work for, deserve — or find yourself. Instead of figuring things out for yourself and trying to help God get the job done, why not concentrate on loving Him, pleasing Him, growing up in Him — and let Him take care of the rest.

> Whoso findeth a wife findeth a good thing, and obtaineth favour of the Lord (Proverbs 18:22).

The Hebrew word for "find" actually means to meet or to have someone appear to you. Some Christians even read this verse and say, "Yeah, well, I found a wife one time, and she wasn't such a hot thing!" But this verse is not saying that just any woman you meet will be a good wife.

A better translation of this verse would be, "Whoever meets a *good* wife finds a good thing, and obtains the grace of God." A good wife or husband is as much a gift of God's grace to you as the new birth or revelation of His Word. A *good* wife or husband is the one He sends.

The Septuagint, which is the Greek translation of the Hebrew Old Testament, adds to this verse by saying, "He that divorces a good wife, divorces a blessing; and takes an unchaste and stupid woman to his bosom." If you get rid of a good wife, you may never have another one who is as good. But if you've found a good wife and rejoice with her as long as you both live, then you've found the grace of God! ✒

FOUR

HUSBANDS, LOVE YOUR WIVES

Like many men, my idea of a good wife was someone who met my needs. She was the one who cleaned the house, did the laundry, cooked the food, raised the kids and did whatever else seemed to go with running the home. Since I have always been good at delegating, it was great telling Loretta what to do!

Of course, I approached my sexual needs in the same way. I thought all I had to do was say a few kind words, kiss her, touch her in the right spots, and within minutes we would have great sex. I thought of her the way you might think of a slot machine — just put in your quarter, pull the handle, and you hit the jackpot!

I don't think I need to tell you the result — not much better then most slot machines! I could not understand why she was not aggressive or enthusiastic about love-making. Still, after I was gratified through sex, I was content to put her back in the kitchen, forget that she existed and ignore her until the next time I needed something from her.

It didn't take too long before I began to see that a woman is not a slot machine. I was frustrated that she wasn't passionate or logical the way I wanted her to be. We were still communicating — at least words were being exchanged. We threw words back and forth, and then we threw other things back and forth! The arguments got worse and worse.

I thought Loretta should submit to me without question, but she didn't. I would tell her, "Submit!" But she wouldn't do it. I thought that "Submit!" was my God-given command, but what I learned later was that *submission is a response*.

God has built into the woman a response of submission when she receives love, care and affection from her husband. Obviously, my command of "Submit!" was not backed by any of these. She had nothing to submit to.

To make matters worse, I made my ministry my highest priority. Everything else was secondary. The truth is, my ministry would have been greater if I had allowed her to share in the troubles, the glories and the rewards of the calling.

Although I knew God had spoken to Loretta about my ministry, I didn't care to listen to a thing she had to say and would never take her advice seriously. By this time I was teaching at a Bible school, and I felt I just didn't need her counsel. Most of the time I just tuned her out — until I needed the slot machine!

She gave me advice, and I shoved it aside. But if someone else told me the same thing — someone I considered a spiritual authority — I would receive it. I would come home and say, "You know what Brother Ken said to me today?" And she would say, "I told you that last week!" I would counter, "But this was Brother Ken!"

After a while she felt so low on my list of priorities and so low on the list of people who mattered to me that she wondered if she was really supposed to be my wife. It seemed that all I needed was a cook, a maid and someone to provide sex on demand. Anybody could perform those duties.

My attitude was that I was faithfully showing my love by providing her with a house, a car, food and clothes. So why didn't she understand? I mean, what was her problem?

Turning Point

Finally we were ready to divorce. We had talked about it many times and had come to the conclusion it was the only thing to do. Neither one of us really wanted a divorce, but we could see no alternative. We were both miserable.

I was convinced she wasn't faithfully following after God by supporting her great husband in the ministry. She, on the other hand, could not figure out why I didn't love her, which to her meant I should be willing to forsake everything else and cling to her.

We were attending a meeting in Tennessee where I was one of the speakers when we decided divorce was the only answer. We had agreed she would take one child and I would take the other. She would leave the meeting early and fly home, take one of the kids, and move out of the house. But when the time came for her to go, she just couldn't do it.

She stood at the door as we said good-bye, but she couldn't turn the doorknob. Somehow I couldn't open the door for her either. As we stood there motionless and speechless, there was something on the inside of us that still knew God had put us together.

We remembered how, earlier in our relationship, the Holy Spirit had supernaturally told each of us the same things about our life together. I would tell her that God had told me something, and she would look at me and say that He had just told her the same thing. Now, standing at the door of divorce, we also remembered things promised by God that were yet to come in our marriage and our ministry.

We knew in our spirits God had brought us together, but this knowledge was covered up by so much unforgiveness, so much pride and so much stubbornness that we were each living in our own worlds. We were two separate people living in the same house, sleeping in the same bed, but going in two different directions.

As we stood at the door of that hotel room, unable to make the next move toward divorce, I made one of the most important decisions of my life. It just so happened that our pastor was arriving the next morning to speak at the same meeting, so I decided to call him.

At first Loretta didn't want to talk to him about the terrible mess we had made of our marriage. She was afraid he would tell everyone at church what was going on in our lives. She thought she would not be able to look anyone in the eye anymore without wondering what they were thinking about us. Later we both realized this is one of the strategies Satan uses to keep couples from getting the help they need.

For once I took authority at the right time. I said, "I don't care. I'm going to call him." I picked up the phone. When he answered, I told him Loretta was ready to walk out the door, and I was ready to give up. We had tried and just couldn't make the marriage work, and the only person I felt I could call was him.

He said, "Tell her to hang around one more day."

We sweated out the next day until he arrived. After the evening meeting, we stayed up until three in the morning talking things out with him and his wife. There is one thing I can remember about that night — one idea that stuck with me and changed my life: You cannot change anyone else; you can only change yourself.

We had reached the point where neither of us was willing to change until the other one changed. I had my list, and she had her list. I refused to meet her demands until she met mine, and vice versa. We had pulled at one another for so long that there was nothing left in us to keep going. We were both empty.

Our pastor listened to us and then pointed this out: *Love does not demand or take; love gives.*

He challenged us to see who could give the most to the other, who could love the other more. I had to decide for myself I was going to love her, whether or not she ever changed. She had to decide for herself that she was going to love me, whether or not I ever changed. Neither of us would hold the other to any grand and glorious promises. We would both be consumed with being the husband or wife God wanted us to be to the other.

That night we made up our minds to stop the competition to get the other to change and begin the competition to out-love one another. Our lives were not transformed overnight, but that decision was the turning point. We still had arguments, misunderstandings and objects flying from time to time, but our commitment to each other continued. Slowly but surely we both began to change, and our love for each other grew. Our marriage began to rise from the ashes.

Marriage and the Ministry

Remember how important my ministry was to me? My wife and I had both known we were going to pastor Grace Fellowship three years before I actually stepped into the pulpit. However, at the time I first took the position, we were having all these problems in our marriage. I pastored for six weeks, and they were six of the worst weeks of my life!

I would be inspired in my study time, but when I walked onto the platform to teach, it seemed as if every word I spoke died. Meanwhile, my life at home was a wreck. We didn't understand how God could make us pastors when we couldn't even get along with ourselves!

At the end of this six-week roller-coaster ride, God spoke to me and said, "You're not the pastor." He told me who the pastor was to be — the man who would later help our marriage. Although I was relieved, I was also confused at the same time. For three years we had waited, knowing that God had called us to be pastors — *but for just six weeks?*

To compensate for my great disappointment, I threw myself into my teaching position. It turned out to be one of the best years I spent at the Bible school. The main reason, of course, was that we had finally talked to our new pastor about our marriage and had begun to work things out in our relationship.

When the school year was half over, God spoke to me again that we were going to pastor Grace Fellowship. My reaction was, "No way!" With the memory of that horrendous six weeks still fresh in my mind, I didn't care if I ever pastored again in my life. But God kept prodding me about the position. He worked everything out so that I became the pastor of Grace Fellowship permanently.

What eventually became clear to me was that I had not been an interim pastor as I had thought. The pastor who had helped us straighten out our marriage had been the interim pastor!

God brought him in to help us put our family life in order and to hold the church together until our relationship was solid.

Jesus tells us that a city set on a hill cannot be hidden and that a lamp must be set on a lamp stand so that all the house can be lit by it (Matthew 5:14-15). These words became very personal and very real to me. I knew that the Word of God I taught from the pulpit should be working in my own life and family. I realized I could not minister the life and love of Jesus to my congregation if I could not minister the life and love of Jesus to my own wife and children.

If a man know not how to rule his own house, how shall he take care of the church of God? (1 Timothy 3:5).

This principle is not only for full-time ministers. Every man must live by it, whether he builds houses or performs major surgery, drives a bus or designs skyscrapers.

When your relationship with your wife is solid and strong, your whole life will be successful and exciting. The fulfillment and joy in your home will spill over into the rest of your life. Your light will shine just as brightly in the world as it shines on the lamp stand in your own home.

For the first time in our marriage I began to see my wife was just as much a gift of grace to me as my ministry. God did not call me as a pastor first and a husband second. We were meant to flow together, and I needed her to fulfill my calling. If I had divorced her, I would have divorced a blessing and probably taken a stupid woman in her place, just as Proverbs says.

Whatever God has called you to be, whether a carpenter,

an accountant or a pulpit minister, if you are married, your marriage comes before your profession. Not only that, but your ability to fulfill your calling will be severely hindered if your marriage is not healthy and happy. That's why the Bible says one of the requirements of a bishop or overseer in the local church is that he "ruleth well his own house" (1 Timothy 3:4-5).

So many couples have this backward. They believe the reason their marriage is in trouble is because they don't have the jobs they want. Even if you are not working where you would like to be working, the joy and stability of your marriage can compensate for that lack of professional fulfillment. Also, as you are faithful to God and to your spouse, God will move you into a position, profession or ministry that is fulfilling.

Getting to Know Her

When we were having marriage problems, I did not understand women, and I didn't care to understand them. As far as I was concerned, Loretta lived in her own world. That was fine with me as long as she did what I needed her to do. But the Bible commands husbands to dwell with their wives according to knowledge. In other words, men, you are out of God's will if you are not taking steps to get to know your wife.

> Likewise, ye husbands, dwell with them according to knowledge, giving honour unto the wife, as unto the weaker vessel, and as being heirs together of the grace of life; that your prayers be not hindered (1 Peter 3:7).

Two words in the Greek language are translated "knowledge." The first is *epignosis*. *Epi* means higher, or above; *gnosis* means knowledge. So *epignosis* is the higher knowledge or revelation received through the Holy Spirit concerning God's Word or His will.

In 1 Peter 3:7, however, the Greek word for "knowledge" is *gnosis* — simple, everyday knowledge. Husbands are supposed to live with their wives according to the natural knowledge of them. I don't know that a man can ever fully understand his wife, but even a little knowledge of her can help him to be *understanding*. The New American Standard Bible says, "Live with your wives in an understanding way."

How is your wife like other women? How is she unique? What pleases her, and what irritates her? What does she enjoy doing? What are her weaknesses, and how can you help her overcome them? What are her strengths, and how can you enhance them? Study her, talk to her and observe how she reacts to different people and situations.

The next thing this verse of Scripture says about women is that husbands are to honor their wives as the weaker vessel. This does not mean she is weaker in intelligence or endurance. In fact, there are some jobs women are much better suited to than men. The word *vessel* is referring to the physical body only (see 2 Corinthians 4:7). A woman is physically not as strong as a man (with a few exceptions, of course), and a husband is reminded to protect his wife with his strength.

The husband's strength is for work and for protection, not for bullying and battering.

Peter declares in verse 7 that the wife is the husband's joint heir. Their individual spiritual inheritances are still intact with the Lord, but a new inheritance for *this life* is given when they are joined together. Marriage for believers is something special!

"That your prayers be not hindered" brings us to one of the most important principles to remember about marriage: *The one-flesh relationship is one of the most powerful positions of prayer in which a believer can be placed.*

When the husband loves his wife as Jesus loves the Church, and his wife responds by submitting to him with respect and honor, they enter a place of power in their prayer lives that makes Satan tremble. Deuteronomy 32:30 says that one can chase one thousand [demons], but two can put ten thousand to flight. In this world, husbands and wives need the power of prayer to maintain a great marriage relationship.

But, husbands, you will not enjoy the victories through unity in prayer if you don't take time to get to know your wife.

Most engaged couples think the way Loretta and I used to think: When you get married, everything comes naturally. But this is not true. Why? Because we are clothed with flesh that is corrupted from the fall of Adam and Eve, and what "comes naturally" is not always right. We must learn to live together *God's way.*

When you were born again, you didn't just naturally know how to worship the Lord, how to love Him, how to please Him and how to walk with Him. You had to study your Bible, pray and learn about these things from your pastor and other believers.

The same is true for marriage. I found that God had a lot to say about my wife to help me understand her better. He also had a lot to say about me and what a husband was supposed to be. I also read books on marriage by other believers and received wise counsel from our pastor and his wife.

Many men give in to pride and refuse to admit they need help to have a successful marriage. To them, studying and learning about marriage is for wimps, those who are "less than a man." Men, don't be embarrassed to let your wife know you are reading books to help you be a better husband and father!

A wife respects her husband when he boldly meets his responsibilities and courageously deals with problems according to the Word of God. She will admire and love you all the more for having the guts to learn about the most important and sensitive issues of your life.

Five Things I Learned About Women

From my study I have learned that a woman looks at marriage and her relationship with her husband differently from how a man does. As a result, her needs vary from her husband's. There seem to be five primary needs that a woman looks to her husband to meet. A husband must be aware of and understand these needs to aggressively love his wife the way Jesus loves us.

1. A wife needs *companionship.* Have you ever noticed that hermits are seldom, if ever, women? That's because women, for the most part, are more sociable than men. When a woman gets married, she views the relationship as lifelong companionship. On the other hand a man sees certain times for companionship in marriage, but then he wants to be alone for a while, work on his car or spend time with the guys.

I'll tell you how important it is for a man to be his wife's companion. Under the Old Testament law, when a man got married, he took a year off and did nothing but spend time with his bride (see Deuteronomy 24:5). How would you like a year-long honeymoon to do nothing but get to know your wife?

When a man comes home from work after being around people all day, he usually wants some peace and quiet. He may want to read the paper or glue himself to the television. But his wife may have been with toddlers all day, talking baby talk, changing diapers and cleaning up messes. When her husband comes home, she wants some companionship! She wants him to sit down, talk to her about his day and listen to her talk about her day.

Sometimes she won't need you to talk or listen; she

just wants you to be there with her. Instead of watching television or reading the paper in the living room, play with the baby in the kitchen while she's fixing dinner. On Saturday, find a neighbor or a friend to watch the kids while you take her shopping or go to a movie.

It's important for her to know that, other than the Lord, you want to spend time with her more than anyone else.

Take her out to dinner regularly, and if you can't afford an expensive place, go to a fast-food place. She'll love it! Ride bikes together, or if you can't afford bicycles, then take walks together. Use your imagination — that's why God gave it to you. There are ways of having time together that are fun and give you time to talk without spending a lot of money.

Traditionally, we have "women's work" and "men's work," but I have found the wife can help her husband with his work and a husband can help his wife with hers. When I mow the lawn, my wife is right out there with me. She does the edging and pulls the weeds, and it is something she likes to do with me. And to my amazement, my masculinity doesn't suffer if I help her with the dishes!

Most important, tell your wife how you feel about her. Tell her you love her. Get rid of your macho pride and let her know what's in your heart.

All these things are even more important if your wife works outside the home. If she is helping to bring in finances, you should help with the children and the housework. And it seems that wives derive the utmost pleasure from talking with their husbands at the end of a busy day, even if they themselves have been around lots of people all day.

Some men have jobs that require them to travel a lot. They can be daily companions to their wives through phone calls, letters or even faxes. However, if the time away is causing serious problems, I encourage them to pray for a job that will keep them at home, or take some time off and do something else for a while in order to work things out. Jobs can come and go, but you want your wife to stay!

A husband needs to understand his wife's desire for companionship and work with her. A wife needs to understand her husband's need for time alone or for hobbies and work with him also. Whatever the circumstances, a strong marriage is give-and-take. Each partner must consider the other and the calling God has placed on their lives.

2. A wife needs *compassion*. Women have a built-in compassion men don't have. Most of the time I slept through the crying of our children in the middle of the night, but Loretta was wide awake at the first whimper. She sees people who are helpless, and her heart goes out to them. Instead, I just wonder why they are in that situation and what could get them out of it. While women are looking for someone who needs help, men are looking for something to help them!

Because a woman has this compassion inside of her and she is giving so much, there are times when she will go through a mood. She may cry, be unusually quiet or become extremely angry over something insignificant. When you ask her what is wrong, she says, "Nothing," or that she doesn't know. This is not the time to analyze and be logical.

She needs her husband to show her compassion. Put your arms around her and hold her. In this way, your compassion for her is replenishing hers. Pray for her and ask for the Holy Spirit to comfort her. There may be something the Lord wants to say to her or minister to her through you.

3. A wife needs *romance*. Women are romantic at heart. Deciding which movie to see is always a challenge because my wife and daughter want to see one with some

romance in it, but my son and I want to see one with a lot of action.

Because a woman is romantic, dating and courtship do not end with the marriage vows. They continue for the rest of your lives. She needs evenings — and a regular vacation — away from the kids, enjoying your undivided attention. She needs to receive cards and flowers once in a while, for no other reason than that you were thinking of her and wanted to show her how you appreciate her. After all, you were her knight in shining armor who came and carried her away. Don't drop her a mile down the road!

It doesn't take a lot of money to be romantic. Just holding her hand or putting your arm around her as you walk can mean a lot. Open doors for her and treat her like a queen in all the little things you do for her.

Giving her presents on her birthday and your anniversary is important, but it's the everyday, little romantic things you say and do that will keep her batteries charged. Then, when you can afford to give her something expensive, she won't feel like you're making up for not paying any attention to her in the past. She'll appreciate the big things more when you take time to do the little things.

4. A wife needs *affection*. Affection is what lets her know that you are protecting her. It gives her a sense of security in your faithfulness and love. Holding her hand, sitting close to her, putting your arm around her whenever possible and touching her gently and often assures her that your strength and love are guarding her.

Affection is more than just touching, however. You can also be affectionate with your words. She needs your encouragement and appreciation for all she is and does. When she's caught in a dilemma and asks for your help, she needs your attention, your prayers and some wise counsel.

Jesus washes the Church with His Word (Ephesians

5:26). So when your wife needs help in some area, take the time to speak uplifting words to her instead of ignoring her or buying her affection with gifts. When we feel lonely or have a problem to work out, isn't it nice that Jesus doesn't just drop a car in our driveway and say, "Here, that ought to make you feel better"?

Our security comes from knowing our relationship with the Lord is a first priority with Him. When we feel His presence, peace and love fill our souls. Your wife's security comes from knowing that, other than the Lord, she is your favorite person. And when you give her your full attention, touching her affectionately, her heart is secure and content.

5. Finally, a wife needs *passion.* Ah! You were hoping I would include that one! But this is very important: If you don't give her the first four — companionship, compassion, romance and affection — you can forget about number five. Remember, she's the well that needs to be stirred up. She's not like you, the fountain, who is always ready to go!

Making love to your wife begins when you get up in the morning, not when you go to bed at night.

If you've spoken encouraging and uplifting words to her during the day, if you've spent time with her, if you've held her hand and opened the door for her, by the time you get to the bedroom, it won't be hard for her to give herself to you and return your passion. Not only will you satisfy her and meet her needs, but *your* satisfaction will be greater.

Because women are not like men in their sex drives, many husbands make the mistake of assuming their wives have no sex drive at all. But this is not true. Your wife wants you to pursue her and stir her up. She enjoys the chase! She looks forward to and enjoys the intimacy and pleasure of lovemaking when you treat her as the special creature God made her to be.

What's a Wimp?

There are two kinds of wimps: the *domineering* husband who refuses to listen to anything his wife says and the *dominated* husband who does everything his wife demands. Most men picture a wimp as the latter — a husband who lets his wife's every whim be his command. But it is equally as weak for a man to have no respect or consideration for his wife's ideas, advice and counsel. God talks to her, too!

You show your love for her by spending time with her and talking *with* her — not acting as if you are listening and then grunting or nodding at appropriate moments. Most important, you show your love for her when you share yourself with her. A woman can cheerfully overcome all kinds of hardship through the years if you share your life with her instead of shutting her out every time something happens.

Some men think that a woman's desire to share every part of their lives is suffocating, but this thinking shows their own ignorance. In reality, a mature Christian woman doesn't want to rule or dominate her husband. She was designed by God to look to him as the head of the home. When you exercise your God-given authority, you provide security and comfort. It makes her insecure and destroys her trust in you if you continually allow her or force her to make decisions that are yours to make.

That doesn't mean your wife doesn't want to be a part of the decision-making process. You may you agree with her, or you may change your mind after hearing her opinion, and that's okay. The final decision is still yours. In most marriages where the husband shares his concerns and considers his wife's counsel, the wife has no problem with her husband's authority.

Your wife wants to be your partner in life, not a compartment of your life.

She does not want to run the show, but merely wants to be a part of the process. And her desire for you to share your innermost thoughts and feelings with her is not a suffocating thing! This is God's provision of emotional freedom for you. She is your best friend, the one to whom you can bare your soul and not be afraid of being exposed to the world. Remember, she is your rib, the hidden strength and support of your life.

A man who has the emotional security of a full, open and honest relationship with his wife is never a wimp. He will walk confidently and boldly as the head of his household. In every area of responsibility he holds inside and outside the home, he won't feel the need to go around proving his manhood. His manhood is already *established* in his relationship with the Lord and *confirmed* in his relationship with his wife.

Who Goes First?

> Wives, submit yourselves unto your own husbands, as unto the Lord. For the husband is the head of the wife, even as Christ is the head of the church: and he is the saviour of the body. Therefore as the church is subject unto Christ, so let the wives be to their own husbands in every thing. Husbands, love your wives, even as Christ also loved the church, and gave himself for it (Ephesians 5:22-25).

If you read verse 22 and then verse 25, it appears that the wife is to submit to the husband first, and then the husband will love her. However, verse 23 says that the husband is the head of the wife in the same way Jesus is the head of the Church, and verse 25 says the husband should love the wife as Jesus loves the Church and gave His life for her.

Did we submit to the Lord first, or did He love us and lay down His life for us first? The book of 1 John gives us the answer: "We love him, because he first loved us" (4:19). Therefore, the husband is to love the wife first — he is the initiator — and the wife is to respond by submitting to his love.

The husband is the aggressor; the wife is the responder.

I love the Lord because He first loved me. He is the aggressor in our relationship by loving me, providing for me, saving me and delivering me. Moreover, He did all these things when I was not worthy. I was lost in my trespasses and sins, separated from God and filled with darkness. Yet, He did not provide 50 percent and expect me to come up with the other 50 percent. He supplied *all* of my needs according to His riches in glory (Philippians 4:19; 2 Pet. 1:3; Ephesians 1:3-14).

All He requires me to do is to respond to His act of love by believing His promises and submitting to His will for my life. Jesus is the aggressor in love, leadership and blessing. We respond in submission, returning His love in praise, worship and obedience.

It is interesting that in Ephesians 5:25 the Greek word for "love" is *agape,* God's aggressive, unconditional love. In Titus 2:4, however, where the Word of God talks about the younger women learning from the older women how to love their husbands, the Greek word for "love" is *phileo.*

Phileo adds rapport or friendship to the meaning of love. It is impossible to *phileo* someone who does not seek out a relationship with you. There must be a friendly exchange of communication and affection. In this sense, the word *phileo* denotes a love which is responsive. Women are taught how to respond (*phileo*) to the aggressive, unconditional love (*agape*) of their husbands.

Likewise, the husband should be the aggressor in more than just sex. He is to be aggressive in loving his wife, caring for her, appreciating her and protecting her. As he gives his life for her, she is secure and free to submit to him as her lord and friend.

> Husbands, love your wives, even as Christ also loved the church, and gave himself for it; that he might sanctify and cleanse it with the washing of water by the word, that he might present it to himself a glorious church, not having spot, or wrinkle, or any such thing; but that it should be holy and without blemish. So ought men to love their wives as their own bodies. He that loveth his wife loveth himself (Ephesians 5:25-28).

A husband is to love as Jesus loves. That means to love, protect and provide for his wife — whether she keeps the house clean or not! Jesus supplies all our needs because He has a giving heart, not because we are perfect all the time.

Furthermore, one of the most important roles a husband plays in the home is found in verse 26: spiritual leadership. As in other areas, God's plan is for him to be the aggressive one. The husband should initiate Bible study, prayer and worship times in the same way he initiates sex.

It seems that in most marriages I have observed, the wife is more spiritually mature and enthusiastic about the things of God than the husband. However, there are cases where the husband is frustrated because his wife is not as spiritually minded as he is.

Jesus is the husband's example, and the Church, which He is sanctifying and cleansing through His Word, is not perfect. There have always been believers who are unwilling to be sanctified and cleansed. Yet Jesus continues to love, protect and instruct us to the degree we will allow Him.

If a husband imparts the Word of God to his wife with

love and affection, he makes it easier for her to choose to receive his spiritual leadership. Even if she is not as "on fire for God" as he is, his love and care for her can touch her heart and inspire her to grow in the Lord.

The Word is likened to a rock in order for us to stand confidently upon it, not to throw it at each other! And in Ephesians 5:26, where God's Word is likened to water, it is not to drown your wife in a torrent of preaching but to refresh her and renew her desire for the truth.

Dating Is for Marriage

We have seen how dating the woman you are going to marry wins over her soul — her emotions, her affections and her thinking. Then when you are married she will freely give you her body. Nevertheless, this does not mean you've finally won the big prize and now you can forget about her soul.

I mentioned this before, and I believe it bears repeating: Dating does not stop after you are married. In fact, dating intensifies because marriage is not built on sex any more than your relationship before marriage was built on sex.

Your friendship is the foundation for your marriage.

God has designed marriage so that the intensity of sex decreases in old age, but love and understanding increase without end. Men, if you marry just for looks and sex, you will be miserable. Marry her because she is the one God has brought to you, the one with whom you want to share your life. Then you will reap the greatest blessings in your later years. If you did marry her just for sex, it's never too late to start courting her.

Every year, love and understanding between you and your wife should grow stronger. Then, sex will be increasingly pleasurable. But if sex is all that has been important, and you haven't continued to court her and date her through your marriage, you have a big shock coming as you grow older!

One day you will notice your sexual desire is fading. Then what will you have to share with her? Suddenly you are two strangers just sharing a house. Instead of enjoying her, you turn to golf, a lodge or the church choir. In order to fill the gap in her life, she takes up bridge and goes on shopping sprees. (There you have it, men. If you want to eliminate shopping sprees, date your wife!)

Remember: The elements of dating and courtship that won her in the first place are what will keep her throughout the years. Getting to know her is a lifelong adventure!

Walking in Covenant

The marriage relationship is a covenant relationship. Our covenant in marriage is patterned after our covenant with God. He gave all He had to us through the cross and the resurrection, and we receive all He has for us when we give everything we have to Him.

In the same way, the husband doesn't have his money and the wife her money; it's their money. Everything he owns is hers, and everything she owns is his. One child isn't his favorite and another child her favorite; all the children are theirs.

We have seen how the power of agreement (see Matthew 18:19) is enhanced between a husband and wife. But so often the husband prays for finances on his way to work, and the wife prays for the children while she's doing laundry. They may continue to struggle in both areas and never have total victory. Though it is good for individuals to pray about areas of concern, how much greater would be the results if husbands and wives joined together in unified prayer!

Christian couples need to understand that every problem which affects them individually affects the marriage. Not only are all of your assets of common interest, but so are all your liabilities. If the husband and wife join together in prayer, agreeing for every need in the family, their unity and combined faith will produce tremendous results. This is living in covenant with each other.

Husbands, you won't walk in this kind of relationship with your wife if you don't take the time to become her friend by spending time with her and talking with her. If she is the most important person in your life other than the Lord, then how bad can it be to spend some time communicating with her?

It is amazing to me that a man will spend hours cleaning his guns or working with his horses but approach his marriage as a spectator instead of a participant. He watches as his wife runs the home and raises the kids, never becoming a part of the home himself. His whole life revolves around his work and his personal interests. When he comes home, he expects his wife and kids to leave him alone and obey every command.

A husband who lives as a dictator and spectator in his marriage is missing the greatest blessings and pleasures of his life. His most prized possession, other than Jesus, is his wife — not his cars and television.

Spending time with your wife and getting to know her means growing up and accepting responsibility. To ignore her is to ignore a large part of your calling in life, which means your ability to prosper in every area of your life will suffer greatly.

If you have children, spend time alone with them, too. Get to know them. Watch your wife fall over in a faint when you come home and announce you are going to establish "Daddy's Night With the Kids" once a week so she can have a night just for herself.

Your kids will get to know you, not just hear about you from their mother. Then when you and your wife pray for your children, you won't feel like an outsider. You'll know what's going on in your family — and it will be a lot easier to explain sex to them when the time comes.

> Be of one mind, live in peace; and the God of love and peace shall be with you (2 Corinthians 13:11).

Covenant relationship is more than sharing all things in common. Covenant relationship is another expression for "one flesh." God designed the husband to initiate the covenant of marriage, just as He initiated our covenant with Him. Then the husband is to continue aggressively pursuing and loving his wife. As he gives all he is and has to her, she will freely give all she is and has to him.

If you honor the marriage covenant by loving your wife as Jesus loves the Church, the two of you will become one in spirit, soul and body. And husbands, the Bible promises that regardless of the challenges and difficulties you face, you will live in peace and God will be with you. ❧

FIVE

WIVES,
SUBMIT YOURSELVES

Ironically, the passion that comes when a man and woman know they are right for one another can only remain strong and continue to grow if they have a proper understanding of submission and authority. This principle is a key to understanding how they are to relate to one another.

The Bible makes it clear that the husband is the head of the home and the wife is to submit to him. But how does this work? With the circulation of feminist ideas in the

Church and so many abuses of "male dominance," most women, even some of the most zealous believers, flinch at the mention of the word *submission.*

The popular perception of submission is that to submit to your husband is to accept an inferior status. When a wife submits, she is declaring herself to be lower than her husband, less intelligent and not as capable as he is. The result is that her entire life and uniqueness are swallowed up in his life.

The popular perception of a husband's authority as head of the home is one of absolute dictatorship without intelligent reason or compassion attached to it. The result is the "macho man" who can have his cake and eat it, too.

But the popular perceptions are not based on God's Word.

We have already seen how the Word of God commands the husband to love his wife aggressively and sacrificially. While he does have final authority in the home, he serves those he leads. Jesus set the precedent when He washed the disciples' feet and declared that the highest in command is the one who is the greatest servant.

Now let's take a look at the true meaning of submission. When a woman understands what God is requiring when He asks her to submit to her husband — and she obeys — she will reach a new level of personal freedom.

Equality

Jesus is Lord — whether we like it or not. The Bible tells us that one day everyone will confess that He is Lord (Philippians 2:11), even those who have rejected Him and are doomed to spend eternity separated from God. But one of the reasons believers freely submit to Him as their personal Lord is that He has seated us with Him in heavenly places (Ephesians 2:6). He has made us joint heirs with Him (Romans 8:17). In other words, He views us as equals.

Although the husband is head of the home, he is not

superior to his wife. Although the wife submits to his final word, she is not inferior to her husband. They are equals.

God has ordained that the principle of submission and authority works only when both those in authority and those in submission recognize the principle of equality. They stand as equals in God's sight. Submission without equality is slavery.

> For the man is not of the woman; but the woman of the man. Neither was the man created for the woman; but the woman for the man (1 Corinthians 11:8-9).

Because the woman was taken from the man, the husband has authority over the wife. But the part of the woman that was constructed from the man was her *body*, not her *spirit*. Her spirit was breathed by God into the body of Adam as a separate entity from Adam's spirit, and she was complete when she was in him.

It was not necessary for Eve to communicate with God through Adam.

A husband is in authority over his wife and is the head of his marriage in all things pertaining to *natural* matters. But in her *spiritual* life, a wife is directly responsible to the Lord Jesus Christ. The husband can never dictate the spiritual activity of the wife. For example, if he does not share her faith in Jesus, he cannot command her not to go to church, pray or read and study her Bible.

A wife in this situation can find rest in knowing she is not being rebellious or out of God's will by continuing to go to church, study the Word and pray.

However, wives, if you want to be a strong Christian witness to your husbands, whether they have accepted Christ or not, make this your attitude: Let your life in God be the *foundation* for all that you do for your husband, not a *conflict*. Then, if any conflict arises because of your commitment to the Lord, it is on His shoulders.

Even if your husband is saved, do not habitually neglect your responsibilities to him and to your family in order to read your Bible, listen to tapes or attend special meetings. This can produce a resentment toward God in your loved ones. Your time in study and prayer should bring balance to your activities and increase your desire to serve others. Draw your strength and wisdom from the Holy Spirit and Scripture in order to be the best wife and mother you can be. By doing this, your family will appreciate and respect your faith.

> Nevertheless neither is the man without the woman, neither the woman without the man, in the Lord. For as the woman is of the man, even so is the man also by the woman; but all things of God (1 Corinthians 11:11-12).

When the husband and wife understand what it means to be in Christ, their equality in Him is clearly established. They have no insecurity about their importance or uniqueness, which is derived solely from God. They have no "axes to grind" or anything to prove to anybody. As a result, authority and submission in the natural things of marriage come easily.

Jesus' teaching caused men and women to view themselves as equals in God's eyes, and this was one of the major controversies of His ministry. Many passages in the Old and New Testaments set the record straight on how God created women and men as spiritual equals, but the strongest of these is found in Galatians.

> There is neither male nor female: for ye are all one in Christ Jesus (Galatians 3:28).

As I have studied the subject of marriage in the Bible, I

have found there are more verses addressing the woman than the man. I believe there is a very good reason for this. Historically, in every society in which Christian principles are not the foundation of the nation, women are not treated with the respect they deserve. Their role in the family, the Church and society at large is grossly misunderstood.

The scriptural view of women is one of the most dramatic aspects of how Christianity impacts a society. From Genesis to Revelation, the Bible declares that spiritually and eternally the woman is equal to the man.

Submission Is an Attitude

Every few years a false teaching arises from Ephesians 5:22: "Wives, submit yourselves unto your own husbands." This false teaching says that wives are to obey their husbands even to the point of violating God's Word. If the husband wants his wife to commit adultery with another man, she is to do it. If he wants her to go to a bar and get drunk with him, she is to do it. Supposedly, her submission will win him to the Lord.

God never requires His children to sin to prove their submissive attitude to Him or to any man.

All false definitions of submission can be put away with the scriptural knowledge and understanding that there is a difference between *submission* and *obedience*. Submission is an attitude; obedience is a deed. You should always *submit* to those in authority over you, although you may not always *obey* them. If someone in authority asks you to do something contrary to the Word of God, you should *submissively decline*.

One biblical example of this is found in Acts 5, where the disciples are brought before the Sanhedrin for preaching the gospel and healing the sick. They did not rebel or fight the Jewish elders when they were arrested, nor did they insult them. They maintained an attitude of submission.

However, when the Sanhedrin ordered them not to preach the gospel or use the name of Jesus again, Peter and the other disciples said, "We ought to obey God rather than men" (Acts 5:29).

Whenever obedience to those in authority would violate God's Word, a believer must respectfully refuse. *This is not the right to rebel against authorities, but God declares that in order to avoid sinning against Him, you may submissively refuse to obey them.*

In essence, submission is humility. Humility, or being humble, is not putting ourselves down, but simply putting others first. If Eve had humbly consulted Adam and the Lord first, she would not have been deceived in the Garden of Eden. Because she acted independently of them, she believed the lie that she could become "as gods" (Genesis 3:5).

The truth is that God and Adam had already made her their queen. It was their authority that had placed her in an exalted position. But Adam also failed to teach her what God had spoken to him in Genesis 2:16-17. Without a sufficient understanding of God's Word, she believed the serpent's lie and placed herself in slavery to Satan by eating the forbidden fruit.

True Freedom

When Eve ate of the tree of knowledge of good and evil, she was deceived. Literally, she believed she would become the Goddess of Earth. Adam, on the other hand, knew exactly what he was doing. He openly rebelled against God when he ate of the same forbidden tree. Because Adam was the head of the family and had been given dominion over the earth, God held him responsible for all sin.

Wherefore, as by one man [Adam] sin entered

into the world, and death by sin; and so death passed upon all men, for that all have sinned (Romans 5:12).

The nature of sin was passed to all men and women from Adam. So God sent Jesus to pay for that sin and thus provide a way back for man to live in His presence.

For as by one man's [Adam's] disobedience many were made sinners, so by the obedience of one [Jesus Christ] shall many be made righteous (Romans 5:19).

The sin of Adam and all its consequences, passed down to us, can be remitted if we receive Jesus Christ as our Lord and Savior. He paid the debt for our sin on the cross and was resurrected from the dead to give us a new spirit, which is filled with God's Holy Spirit. Then, instead of living according to our fleshly nature, we can live according to God's nature in communion with Him.

But how did Eve's role in the fall affect women thereafter? The sin of rebellion that Eve passed down to all women is declared by God in Genesis 3:16. In this verse God tells Eve exactly what she and women after her will reap because she acted independently of His and her husband's authority.

Unto the woman he said...thy desire shall be to thy husband, and he shall rule over thee (Genesis 3:16).

The Hebrew word for "desire" means more than lust or passion. It means "to stretch over" or "run over." The implication is that women will seek to manipulate and rule their husbands. Believing they could do a better job of leading, they will strive with their husbands over every matter.

In the last part of the verse, God reminds Eve that He has not changed His mind about order in the home. Her husband is still the head. What this means is, even though they will seek to rule their husbands — and some may even succeed in doing so — wives will never be able to eliminate the God-given authority of their husbands.

Being spiritually separated from God in the fall, Adam and Eve lost their sense of equality and uniqueness before their Creator. As a result, submission became something the woman resented. She grieved over the loss of her queenly position and the aggressive unconditional love with which Adam used to adore her.

Adam's authority became the dictatorial rule of an insecure man. This man, who had just the day before walked and talked with God in the cool of the day, now blamed his wife for everything. Instead of finding his security and importance in God, he sought to prove himself by taking advantage of the authority God had given him over his wife. Adam was the world's first wimp!

Eve passed two deceptions down to all women: first, that wives could rule over their husbands, and, second, that women must strive to prove their equality with men. This legacy is the root of all women's movements through the ages. However, the answer is not in a movement, but in the person of Jesus Christ.

When we submit ourselves to Jesus as our personal Lord and Savior, He gives us new spirits which can communicate directly with God. Instead of striving to rule over or outdo others to prove our worth and importance, we receive our value and the unconditional love we crave from Him.

We are free in Jesus Christ — to love and serve others out of the limitless supply of God's love in our hearts.

Because true liberation for women comes only through submitting their lives to Jesus Christ, you could say that the real women's liberation movement began with Jesus' ministry. Some of His greatest supporters were women:

Mary and Martha, Mary Magdalene, the woman at the well, and his own mother, Mary.

Carrying this one step further, true freedom for a wife comes through submitting to her husband.

Unfortunately, the modern feminist movement has painted a very bleak picture of what a submissive wife is — mindless, with no personality or individuality, and completely dominated by her husband. She has no sense of who she is; she is merely her husband's wife.

Taken to the extreme, this view of a submissive wife is one who can be raped in the bedroom and beaten in the kitchen because she is in bondage to the "traditional" view of what a wife is.

It is true that many men have abused their wives throughout history. It is also true that abuse occurs when God's truth about marriage is not known and applied. The biblical picture of a submissive wife is a very different one from that of the women's liberation movement.

> Wives, submit yourselves unto your own husbands, as unto the Lord. For the husband is the head of the wife, even as Christ is the head of the church: and he is the saviour of the body. Therefore as the church is subject unto Christ, so let the wives be to their own husbands in every thing (Ephesians 5:22-24).

The kingdom of God is directly opposed to the kingdom of Satan. In Satan's realm, exalting yourself is supposed to bring you fulfillment, and being your own god is supposed to bring you happiness. But in God's realm, He is your sufficiency in all things. As you humble yourself, He will exalt you at the perfect time (1 Peter 5:6).

In Satan's world you are focused on yourself, ignoring the reality of God's ultimate authority, rising or falling by your abilities and talents, and trusting in your own understanding. In God's kingdom you are focused on Jesus, fulfilled and made whole through His love, joyfully submitted to and trusting in His will, and success is measured by your obedience to Him in blessing others.

> He that findeth [holds onto] his life shall lose it: and he that loseth his life for my sake shall find it (Matthew 10:39).

The true freedom women (and men) long for is found only by losing themselves in Jesus Christ and thereby discovering — and becoming — whom they really are.

A wife's freedom is multiplied by submitting to her husband as well as to the Lord Jesus Christ. She gains twice the protection and blessing. God would not ask her for increased submission without giving increased reward. This is a supernatural law! The freedom of loving unconditionally is multiplied to the submissive wife.

The Power of Submission

Where God has given a husband *authority* in marriage, He has given a wife *power*. This power comes from her attitude of submission to her husband. When a wife approaches her husband with a humble attitude of honor and respect, when her sole desire in their relationship is to please him in any way she can, he can become clay in her hands!

To avoid abusing this power, wives should understand the difference between *influence* and *manipulation*. The difference is found in the motivation of her heart. When a wife obeys but her heart is in rebellion or she gives advice meant to manipulate, she is perverting her God-given female power over her husband in order to get him to do what she wants him to do. When she submits inwardly in order to influence him, she is turning her husband over to

God. Then the Holy Spirit can work freely in her husband's life.

Wives, as you submit yourselves to your husbands, the power of God is on the scene to answer your prayers!

> Likewise, ye wives, be in subjection to your own husbands; that, if any obey not the word, they also may without the word be won by the conversation of the wives; while they behold your chaste conversation [manner of life] coupled with fear [respect] (1 Peter 3:1-2).

"Likewise" means the Holy Spirit has not changed the subject from the previous chapter, where Peter exhorted believers to submit to the authorities in their lives — whether they are fair or unfair.

In the same manner that you are salt and light in your job, you are a witness in the home. Just as you submit yourself to the authority of your employer, who may be unreasonable and unjust, you submit to the authority of your husband.

As Jesus committed Himself to the Father before unreasonable men, wives should commit themselves to God and trust Him as they live godly lives before their husbands. When they do this, the Holy Spirit moves powerfully through their lives. There is tremendous power in submission!

Before I go any further, I want to comment on the danger of taking these verses to an extreme. In many cases of physical abuse, a Christian wife uses these verses to justify being beaten by her husband. She believes that enduring the battering of her husband is a witness to the power of God's love, and that by submitting to her husband's abuse, he will come to obey the Word of God.

This is not what these verses are saying! It is never God's will for you to be physically abused by your husband. We will discuss this subject in more detail in chapter 8.

For the most part, it is easy for a wife to submit to the Lord because He is perfect, long-suffering and totally trustworthy. It is more difficult to submit to an imperfect human being, whether it is your boss or your husband. However, God's Word commands it, and He promises sufficient grace for you to do so.

When you step out in faith in any situation, and you know you are in the will of God, you have the peace and confidence of knowing He will reward you. When a wife submits to her husband in faith, she is honoring God. The Bible says that those who honor God by obeying Him in faith, He will honor (1 Samuel 2:30).

> Likewise, ye wives, be in subjection to your own husbands; that, if any obey not the word, they also may without the word be won by the conversation of the wives; while they behold your chaste conversation [manner of life] coupled with fear [respect]" (1 Peter 3:1-2).

This verse commands a wife to submit to her husband even if he does not obey the Word. Although the phrase "if any obey not the word" refers to an unbelieving husband, the same wisdom applies to a Christian husband who is backslidden or carnal. A wife can influence her husband to obey the Word of God by her "conversation," or manner of life.

I used to wonder why a word meaning "manner of life" was translated *conversation*. One day the Holy Spirit spoke to me and said, "Your actions speak." You communicate by the words of your mouth and *by the way you live your life*. We witness for the Lord by word and deed (Colossians 3:17).

The Holy Spirit was given to us so we can *be* a witness, not *do* witnessing (Acts 1:8). This same principle applies to marriage. Your husband can be more easily won by your submissive attitude and consequent actions than by nagging and preaching.

Often when a wife advances in her spiritual life, she loses respect for her husband because he doesn't seem to care about the Lord with the same intensity she does. However, this attitude of disrespect goes against what 1 Peter teaches.

A wife is to respect and submit to her husband because he is her husband, her grace gift from God, not because he is where she wants him to be spiritually.

A submissive attitude is powerful because by it you are showing your husband the unconditional love God has for him. Regardless of his attitude, regardless of his faults or mistakes, you are treating him with honor and respect.

First Peter 3:2 says that your husband is watching you and your way of life. He may act as if he's ignoring you, but the Holy Spirit says he is watching you! It is his pride that is causing him to deny it.

He notices your respect for him as head of the home. He sees how the Lord helps you and sustains you through difficult situations. He can't help but notice the joy and inner peace your faith brings, and the unmistakable honor and power God gives you as you submit to him.

If a wife has a rebellious, unsubmissive attitude toward her husband, she takes matters into her own hands and cuts off the move of the Holy Spirit in her marriage. On the other hand, submitting to her husband allows the Holy Spirit to open his heart and mind to God. Then God can deal with him about his life. Whether he needs to be saved, filled with the Holy Spirit or set free in an area of carnality, a submissive wife releases the power of God into her husband's life.

Divine Order in the Home

The power of God cannot flow in the absence of divine order. Everything God does is good, and everything He does reflects His perfect, orderly way of thinking. His ways and thoughts are not random and scattered, but structured and filled with purpose. Therefore, when He put more than one human on earth, He established a chain of command to avoid confusion and every evil work.

Spiritually speaking, we are all equal. In natural things, God has ordained a chain of command in government (Romans 13:1-6), in the universal Church (Ephesians 4:11-12), in the local church (Hebrews 13:7,17) and in the family (1 Corinthians 11:3). In His wisdom, He did this to maintain order and provide protection and security.

When practiced, the principle of authority and submission allows us to carry out our lives in freedom and safety.

In the Book of Ephesians, for example, the first half of the book discusses in depth our position in Christ, establishing that we are all equal before God. The second half of the book then tackles submission and authority in every relationship, from government and citizen to husband and wife. These principles were not meant to put one person in bondage to another, but to provide order and protection in all levels of society.

God has set up a chain of command in the family as well. Man originally came from God, then the woman came from the man. Children, including male children, are born from women (see 1 Corinthians 11:11-12, Amplified). A young boy first learns authority by submitting to the authority of his mother. How a boy learns to treat his mother determines how he will treat his wife.

It is important for a mother to train her son to become a gentleman before he is old enough to use his strength abusively. She must teach him to channel his energy and strength in the right way and discipline him to respect her. Then he will respect all women.

She must teach him that what a mature woman is looking for in a man is not muscles, an expensive car or a high position in society. Those things are fine, and they are blessings, but they are not the highest on her list. What she is looking for is a gentleman, someone who will open doors for her, pull out her chair for her, and treat her like the prized possession she is. Since God took more time with her than He did with the man, and He created her in an entirely different manner from any other creature, she wants a husband who knows how special she is.

A boy also needs to learn by example from his father. The boy might play sports with his dad and see him hit a baseball out of the park. He knows his dad could pick anybody up and throw them across the room if he wanted to. But when his father comes home, instead of using his strength against his mother, he puts his arms around her, loves her and protects her.

The same principle holds for intellectual strength. His father may be highly intelligent and quick-witted. But instead of being quick to criticize his mother, the boy sees his father use his mind to please her, to encourage her, to help her solve problems and to make her laugh.

The boy can see that strength — both physical and intellectual — is not only for making a living, but for protecting and loving the family, too. He also watches his father's whole being melt with one or two words from his mother! He realizes the power God has given the woman over the man, and he respects his mother for her wisdom in using that power for his dad's benefit. Most important, he sees the tremendous love his parents have for each other.

Just as the son learns how to love his wife by observing his father and mother, a daughter learns how to submit to her husband by watching her mother and father as well. As she sees her mother respond to her father's love by honoring and respecting him, she will find joy in being a wife herself one day. She learns about the power she has over her husband and the necessity to avoid abusing that power.

Because she has seen her father aggressively and unconditionally love her mother, she will not chase boys or be promiscuous. One of the major symptoms that demonstrates that male/female relationships have been turned upside down is women pursuing men. This generally does not occur when a girl grows up observing how her father is the aggressor in love, protection and provision. She is not driven to find a man and trap him, but is content to wait for God to bring the right one. Instinctively, she knows that any man she has to chase is not worth having.

The home is the classroom and laboratory where children grow up to become successful or unsuccessful husbands and wives. When a boy sees his father abuse his mother, verbally or physically, and hears words like, "Never trust a woman," he learns insecurity and confusion. Unless Jesus Christ changes him, a boy with this kind of upbringing can end up fornicating in high school and eventually in the office, too. He will cheat on his wife if he ever gets married and will probably abuse her as well.

Unless Jesus Christ changes her, a girl who grows up watching her mother dominate, manipulate and disparage her father will treat her husband the same way. She will never know a day of peace in marriage and will probably be married many times — or forsake the institution altogether for a series of "relationships."

We spend so much time and money buying things for our children that we often overlook the most valuable possession we can give them — the daily example of a godly marriage. Then when your child finds the right mate and the apron strings are cut, you can have peace and confidence that they will have a great marriage, too.

The divine order God has set in the home begins with the relationship between the husband and wife — he as head, she as his equal partner but second-in-command.

The children learn authority and submission from their parents. Until a child learns how to submit to his parents, he will not understand what it means to be in authority.

> Humble yourselves therefore under the mighty hand of God, that he may exalt you in due time (1 Peter 5:6).

Children learn humility as they are trained and taught by their parents and as they learn to submit to their authority. The best leaders are the most submissive followers. How high do you want to climb? *How low are you willing to serve?*

Handling Conflict

If children see divisiveness between their parents, they will try to take advantage of them to get their way. For instance, a child goes to Mom and asks for a cookie, but Mom says, "No, it's too close to dinner." So the child goes to Dad and asks the same thing, and Dad says, "OK with me." A few minutes later Mom sees the child eating the cookie in the backyard. When she calls him on it, the child replies, "Dad said I could."

It's time for Dad to call a family meeting! He says, "Kids, you are never to pit Mom and Dad against each other. I'm changing my answer to no because Mom said no in the beginning."

In this example the husband took responsibility for the situation as head of the family, considered his wife's counsel and made a decision that agreed with her. If, however, he had decided to overrule his wife's decision, what should she do?

If he is not violating the Word of God or causing his children to sin, she should abide by his decision. Her submissive and forgiving attitude will turn him completely over to the Holy Spirit. And the Holy Spirit has a way of changing someone's mind when no other person can get through! More than that, she is showing her children what to do when "it isn't fair" but there is no violation of God's Word that requires protest or disobedience.

If the husband is in violation of Scripture, she must say, "George, I love you, and you are a good man, but the Bible says I cannot do this." George may be a little upset, but because her attitude honors him as well as God, he will be more inclined to listen to the Holy Spirit.

Where there is divine order, there is divine power.

If you disagree about something or are about to have a "heated discussion," it is wise to go someplace private. However, if you do disagree in front of the children, make sure they see that you resolve the conflict with affection and forgiveness. (You will have to crucify some flesh!)

Even in cases where a husband and wife cannot reach an agreement, the children should see how you can disagree without being disagreeable. (More flesh must go on the cross!) This teaches them the scriptural way to handle conflict in their own lives. It also makes them unafraid to face conflict and disagreement later on in their adult lives.

Where there is divine order, there is security.

When children know their parents are unified, that Dad is in charge but Mom is his chief counselor, peace reigns in the home. But this is impossible when the mother has a rebellious attitude toward the father. When she usurps her husband's authority, the children will try the same with her. Many cases of rebellion in youth today can be traced to the lack of respect the mother had for the father.

Even in homes where the father is an unbeliever or is not loving his wife as Scripture commands, the security of God's divine order can still prevail if she has an attitude of submission and respect for her husband (see 1 Corinthians 7:14). This is a difficult place for a wife to stand, but God will give her grace and strength equal to the challenge.

How often do we hear parents say, "I just want a better world for my child." The truth is that we can never make a better world for our children. Jesus said that the world is going to get worse (Matthew 24:4-8). What we can do is make better children for the world by providing homes where divine order is followed.

Understanding Male Aggression

Just as there were things about women that I had to understand in order to love my wife, there were some things about men that Loretta had to understand. Again, God made us different in significant ways.

One of a wife's greatest eye-openers comes when she realizes her husband is aggressive. God made him to desire to conquer and subdue, to succeed and prosper. Used in a godly way, these qualities are what enable him to exercise the authority God has given him to provide and protect.

Wives love it when their husband's aggression brings security and prosperity to the home, but they often have trouble when all that drive gets into bed with them! Highly aggressive men have strong sex drives. In fact, much of a man's life is filtered through his sexual identity. One of a man's greatest challenges in the Christian life is controlling sexual urges and remaining holy. Even in marriage he must guard against using his authority to take advantage of his wife sexually.

A wife's challenge is to understand her husband's sex drive and flow with it. Some wives come to me and announce that their husbands are perverted or sex-crazed because they want to have sex every night. They need to know that a man seeks daily fulfillment in an intimate relationship with his wife in the same way he seeks daily fulfillment from his profession or anything else he pursues.

At this point many women feel manipulated. Some, because of sexual abuse or promiscuity in their past, may see men through the eyes of mistrust and fear. But the one-flesh relationship requires the wife to see her husband's point of view in sex. Understanding and accepting your husband's sex drive and passion will only bless you, not destroy you.

That's why knowledge of God's Word on the subject of sex is so important, because the Word exhorts you to approach all things, including sex, through faith and not fear. Faith comes from knowledge, and fear comes from a lack of it. Thus, understanding increases love, and mature love casts out fear.

A woman's fear of sex brings on her what she fears most: a desire from her husband for more sex. Many sexually frustrated wives want their husbands to understand their fears in order for the frequency of sex to decrease. However, this will not benefit the marriage, but only worsen an already bad situation.

On the other hand, a wife who decides to respond passionately to her husband's sexual advances will most often find quite a different result. The sexual frequency may increase at the beginning but will later decrease. Each sexual encounter will become more wonderful as he is gratified from her loving willingness and submission.

Women, you have no idea how wonderful marriage can be until you see a sexually gratified husband! The benefit to your husband can only benefit you also. A sexually satisfied husband is usually a good provider. He provides for his wife and desires to please her out of appreciation, not obligation. He is less tempted to lust after other women because his thoughts are filled with her.

Essential to understanding a man is understanding his ego. God gave each of us an ego, or a sense of self, so it is not an evil thing unless we allow it to become puffed up in pride, independent of God. A godly ego, or sense of self, is constantly aware that its identity and significance is dependent upon a relationship with the Creator.

Men are little boys in big bodies, and their sensitive area is their ego. At the heart of their ego is the consciousness of their manhood. The husband's manhood should come first of all from his relationship with the Lord Jesus Christ. Then in the marriage relationship his wife should confirm his manhood, not tear it down.

A wife confirms her husband's manhood by showing she is behind him, that she respects him, values him and enjoys it when he makes love to her. She looks forward to, and even plans times when they can be intimate with one another. A man is just a big boy who seeks the respect and godly passion of the woman he loves!

If a wife frequently refuses sex with her husband, making excuses time and again, he begins to feel inadequate. This sense of failure soon extends to other areas of his life, because his wife's continual rejection can warp his sense of self. Only a strong relationship with the Lord can keep a husband's manhood intact when his wife continually refuses to have sex with him.

If his wife only makes love with him out of duty and obligation, she is not pursuing a one-flesh relationship (*proskollao*), she is merely having sex (*kallao*). Her husband can develop an image of himself as less than a man, reduced to the level of animals.

However, when a wife lets her husband know how much she welcomes his aggression and enjoys loving him, it enhances his ego and gives him confidence to accomplish his life's goals. The communication lines with his wife are free and open, and intimacy becomes stronger through the years.

So many women believe the important things in marriage are to keep a clean house, fix good meals, take care of the children, and make sure everything in the home runs smoothly. They will expend incredible energy in these areas and have nothing left when it comes time to go to bed. As a result, they slight their husbands in sex, which to them is one of the most important areas of their relationship.

This does not mean you can justify keeping a sloppy house by never refusing your husband sex! Arrange your activities so you won't be exhausted by bedtime. Remember, your husband will not mind the dishes in the sink for one night if it means he can make love to a responsive, passionate wife.

Everlasting Beauty

All women desire to be beautiful, and all wives desire to be beautiful in their husband's eyes. Christian women go one step further and desire to be beautiful in the eyes of Jesus. But what is it that really makes a woman beautiful?

> I will therefore that men pray every where, lifting up holy hands, without wrath and doubting. In like manner also, that women adorn themselves in modest apparel, with shamefacedness and sobriety; not with braided hair, or gold, or pearls, or costly array (1 Timothy 2:8-9).

Paul is admonishing husbands to walk in sanctification, keeping their hearts full of faith and free of unforgiveness. In the same way that husbands are to maintain a visible life of holiness, women are to "adorn themselves in modest apparel."

Since the beginning of time women have known what their clothing communicates. A woman should remember that how she dresses makes a statement about the Lord Jesus Christ, and how a wife dresses reflects on her husband.

"Modest" simply means proper, not sackcloth and ashes. Modest apparel is anything suitable for you. There is nothing wrong with being fashionable as long as the clothing is not too revealing. You can look great without showing parts of your body meant only for your husband's eyes.

Being raised in the church, I have seen both extremes. I remember women who dressed so plainly they attracted attention to themselves because they looked older than their years. I have also seen women whose dress was so revealing they advertised dissatisfaction with their husbands and sent out the wrong signals.

We are not to attract attention to ourselves but to the Lord Jesus Christ. If you are single and dressing to attract attention to yourself by exposing too much, you will attract the wrong kind of person. They will be drawn to your body, not the real you, and will be more interested in getting you into bed than working on a relationship.

Women are to dress properly, "with shamefacedness and sobriety; not with braided hair, or gold, or pearls, or costly array." This does not mean you should always have a horrible look on your face, be serious and never braid your hair, buy expensive clothes or wear jewelry.

These words could be better translated, "Adorn yourselves with modesty and discretion, not just with physical things like clothes and jewelry and the style of your hair." Outward dress and appearance are important, but God has a beauty plan for the believing woman that no department store or cosmetic line ever dreamed of.

> Whose adorning let it not be that outward adorning of plaiting the hair, and of wearing of gold, or of putting on of apparel; but let it be the hidden man of the heart, in that which is not corruptible, even the ornament of a meek and quiet spirit, which is in the sight of God of great price (1 Peter 3:3-4).

It is the attitude of a woman that makes her beautiful, both to her husband and to the Lord.

The adorning on the inside, in the hidden man of the

heart, is not corruptible but is timeless. On the other hand, jewelry and clothing are corruptible. In twenty years, that designer dress you love today will be frayed and not worth a fraction of its original cost.

If you grow in knowledge and wisdom in your heart, your inward beauty will be seen outwardly and will grow more and more stunning as the years go by. This passage of Scripture tells a wife that a meek (teachable) and quiet (prayerful) spirit is a beautiful ornament to God and to her husband.

An ornament is something we display, something exquisite that we want to show everyone. When a wife submits herself to God and to her husband, concentrating on the development of her heart and mind, her meek and quiet spirit literally adorns her. Her attitude of grace and wisdom becomes more noticeable than her clothing, hairstyle or jewelry. Long after her physical beauty fades, her heart will be an ornament of God's love before the world.

Sarah Called Abraham "Lord" — by Faith

Have you ever been with a couple when the husband is explaining something, and his wife interrupts to correct him? Typically, she breaks in with something like, "No, that's not the way it happened. That was *after* our vacation."

He comes back with, "I beg your pardon, but it was before our vacation," and before you know it they are in a heated argument about something totally insignificant. If the wife remains adamant that she is right, her husband will usually concede to her opinion so he can finish his story.

When a wife continually dominates her husband, in most cases he will become weak in order to "keep the peace." Many dominating wives do not understand how an unsubmissive attitude promotes their husband's weakness.

A dominating wife never submits to her husband or allows him to be the head of the home *because she is afraid that he will make the wrong decisions.* The Bible gives an example of this in 1 Peter 3.

> For after this manner in the old time the holy women also, who trusted in God, adorned themselves, being in subjection unto their own husbands: Even as Sarah obeyed Abraham, calling him lord: whose daughters ye are, as long as ye do well, and are not afraid with any amazement (1 Peter 3:5-6).

The phrase "For after this manner" refers to the first four verses of this chapter in which Peter says that the attitude of a woman's heart, not her outward appearance, ultimately wins the heart and soul of her husband. This passage then talks about Sarah, who called Abraham "lord."

The Bible tells us that Sarah was very beautiful physically, so beautiful that Abraham told her to pose as his sister on two occasions so no one would kill him to have her! (This gives insight into how weak-kneed Abraham was.) Sarah's physical beauty was not giving her a great deal of happiness!

Sarah was originally called Sarai, which means "contention." Today we would use the word *nagging.* Sarai encouraged Abraham to be weak by constantly complaining. Proverbs 27:15 gives wives some practical wisdom about nagging.

> A continual dropping in a very rainy day and a contentious woman are alike.

A wife who nags her husband is like a continual dripping on a rainy day — drip, drip, drip — until nerves finally explode. Wives, this is not the way to be your husband's friend or to change him. All that nagging accomplishes is to cause a husband to become angry, tune out his wife and continue doing whatever was irritating her.

If he does change because of her forcefulness, he will be resentful. The root of the problem is that the relationship is upside down. The wife has become the aggressive one by her nagging, and the husband has become the responder by giving in to her demands. Ultimately he will not feel like a man, and the wife will not feel like a woman.

Sarai was not happy or fulfilled because she was always correcting Abraham and probably tried to usurp his authority in everything. It wasn't until Sarai was ninety years old, after she and Abraham had been married for sixty years and her outward beauty had faded, that "Sarai the Contentious" became "Sarah, the Princess."

On that day, she chose to call Abraham "lord." She chose to submit to him — and she fell in love with him all over again. Not only did she and her husband enter into a new and exciting relationship, but she miraculously conceived Isaac, the child God had promised many years before. I believe that many times when a woman is trusting God for an answer to prayer, the fulfillment of that promise is waiting for the moment when she will recognize her husband as "lord."

Wives, you are the daughters of Sarah "as long as ye do well, and are not afraid with any amazement" This means you live a life pleasing to God and do not fear. As I have said before, submission to Jesus is easy because He is perfect. Submission to an imperfect husband, on the other hand, can cause fear to rise up in a woman. This verse exhorts wives to be like Sarah, to stand up in faith and boldly call their husbands "lord," not letting fear dominate them.

Submission works by faith.

When a wife lets go of fear and embraces faith in God as Sarah did, inner peace reigns in her heart. She understands she is equal with her husband before the Lord. She can then submit to her husband as unto the Lord — by faith.

She respects the role of "head of the marriage" in the same way she reveres the "head of the church."

A woman walks into freedom, joy and fulfillment in her life when she submits to the Lord Jesus Christ. A wife walks into freedom, joy and fulfillment in her marriage when she submits to her husband. In this way, she fully reverses Eve's transgression. What a wonderful paradox! Instead of exalting herself as her own god, independent of the Lord and her husband, she humbly submits herself to them and becomes, in their eyes, a princess!

When a wife submits herself to her husband, the Bible says she becomes his glory (1 Corinthians 11:7), "which is in the sight of God of great price" (1 Peter 3:4). The rewards she receives eternally far outshine and greatly surpass what she has given. Submission is truly a wife's valiant act of faith and worship! ❧

SIX

ARE SINGLES COMPLETE?

Whenever I teach about the marriage relationship, singles get the idea that they have to be married to be complete. But God's Word makes it clear that this is not the case. While you are single, God fills the gap in your life. He becomes your sufficiency.

Furthermore, it is very important that married people honor and respect singles. Married people should not push singles to get married or treat them as if something is wrong because they are not married.

Being married or single is a private matter between a believer and God. If a single person is waiting for the Lord to bring the right person, the last thing they need is for married people to evaluate their spirituality according to whether or not they have a mate. If someone has chosen to remain single, then keep your nose out of his or her business!

Some of the greatest men and women in the Bible were single, including Jesus. I don't believe anyone would say that Jesus, the Apostle Paul or Timothy were unable to serve God or fulfill their ministries because they were single.

Scriptural Guidelines for Dating

The most common question singles ask me is, "What does the Bible say about dating, and what are the guidelines?" We can begin with 1 Corinthians 7:1:

Now concerning the things whereof ye wrote unto me: It is good for a man not to touch a woman.

Obviously, this is a Scripture verse for single people! Taken as it reads, you could assume the Holy Spirit is saying, "Unless you are married to her, don't touch her." However, the meaning of this verse is, "It is not good for a man to *kindle* a flame in a woman." It refers to touching to incite lust.

We have seen in Proverbs 6:27-28, where David instructs Solomon, "Can a man take fire in his bosom, and his clothes not be burned?" that a "flame" indicates sexual passion. These verses are declaring that, outside of marriage, if you stir up the fire, you are going to get burned!

First Corinthians 7:1 clearly holds the man responsible for physical contact in a dating situation.

"It is good for a *man* not to touch a woman." Namely, he should not do anything to her that would arouse her sexual appetite. Proverbs compared the woman to a well of water — and a well is still. It takes time for her to be aroused. Where a man is stimulated by sight, a woman is stimulated by tender words and a soft touch. If a man is touching a woman who is not his wife to kindle a flame, he is out of line with God.

At the same time, a woman should never yield to a man out of pressure or fear she will lose him. If he thinks so little of her that he would compromise her virtue to satisfy his carnal desires, he is not worth having. If he really respects her, he will not try to arouse her sexual desire in the first place. If it should happen, and she tells him to stop, he will respect her for it and apologize for allowing things to get out of hand.

When I teach on marriage, I instruct the younger boys in our congregation to introduce themselves to the parents of the girl they are going to take out in order to establish a relationship of trust with them beforehand. I also instruct them to tell the parents when they plan to have her home and that they will call if they are going to be late. Then I warn them that they might have to pick her father or mother up off the floor because behaving like a gentleman is so rare in our society — especially in young men!

When a boy picks a girl up for a date, he must understand that for the time he is with her, he is the guardian of her soul and the protector of her body. Ultimately he answers not only to her parents but to God. Parents should know the boy whom their daughter is going out with or the girl whom their son is dating.

The same guidelines hold true for older men and women. The man may not be answering to his date's parents, but he is still accountable to God for his treatment of her.

I always caution singles to get to know people of the

opposite sex in group situations, with friends or with family, before spending any time alone with them. Be certain their values are the same as yours, even if you consider them just friends. And when you do spend time alone together, make sure it is in a situation where there is little temptation to get into sexual activity.

Although it is not mentioned in this verse, the woman also has a responsibility not to arouse the man. Remember how the Bible compares the man to a fountain? Just the sight of a woman can get him going! That's why 1 Timothy 2:9 directs women to dress modestly. How you dress can determine how he treats you.

This also applies to promiscuous talk and behavior. Even if a woman dresses modestly, if she acts and talks seductively, her date's focus is going to be toward her body and not her mind and heart. If he is a godly man, he should drop her like a hot potato. If he is not a godly man, he will aggressively pursue the physical relationship because she is giving him all the signals to go ahead.

> Nevertheless, to avoid fornication, let every man have his own wife, and let every woman have her own husband (1 Corinthians 7:2).

The word *own* constitutes the foundation for a single person's sexual behavior. In marriage you *belong* to each other and no one else. Marriage is a type of the Church being joined to Jesus. In Christ we are not our own; we belong to Him. When you are married, you belong to someone; you are no longer your own. You are to love and please your partner in the same spirit you love and please the Lord.

That is why it is so important not to "kindle a flame" while you are dating. You belong only to your future spouse. When the right one comes along, you will be very glad that you put out the fire inside and kept yourself from burning.

You don't want to smell like smoke on your wedding day!

The admonition "to avoid fornication" brings out another aspect of dating. The longer you date, the more difficult it will become to keep from getting involved sexually. I don't believe it is God's will for a couple to date for years. If you have had enough time to recognize that God brought you together for marriage, and if you have dated long enough to know each other, get married! If you are not dating the right person, and there is any physical attraction at all, break it off now. Quit playing with fire!

A fire that burns uncontrollably causes damage and destruction. But a fire contained within boundaries is a blessing. A forest fire leaves the land desolate, but a fire in the fireplace gives warmth. In the same way, the flame of godly passion was put there by God, but it needs to be confined within the boundaries of marriage to be a blessing.

Whenever anyone tries to pin me down about rules and regulations regarding physical contact in dating, I tell them this: Don't stir the fire. With most couples, it doesn't take a lot of physical contact to kindle the flame. There are some who just look at each other and can hardly keep from jumping into bed. Others can kiss and walk away from each other — using much self-control.

It comes down to two things. First, be honest with yourself about your weaknesses and keep yourself from tempting situations. Second, always remember that your body belongs to your future spouse. Don't do anything on a date that you would not feel comfortable telling your husband or wife about later.

The Question You Always Wanted to Ask

There is one question I am always asked in letters but rarely in person: What does the Bible say about masturbation? Most Christian books say that God's Word is silent about the subject, but that is not true.

> The wife hath not power [authority] of her own body, but the husband: and likewise also the husband hath not power [authority] of his own body, but the wife (1 Corinthians 7:4).

Our society teaches that masturbation is a normal release for sexual pressure. It is a way of discovering your own sexuality and finding out what pleases you. But God says this is the exclusive right of your future or present mate. Men, you do not have sexual authority over your own body. Your wife does. Women, you do not have sexual authority over your own body. Your husband does.

Singles, if you choose to be married one day, your future mate has authority over your body sexually. You are to focus your thoughts on the Lord and keep yourself pure until marriage. After marriage, your sex drive will be directed toward loving and pleasing your spouse, not yourself. If you choose to remain single, God gives grace to remain sexually pure as you devote yourself to serving Him.

Masturbation is a selfish act to satisfy your flesh for the moment, and it is not condoned by the Word of God. It is an indulgence of the flesh. The more you indulge the flesh, the more you will think, talk and act according to the flesh. In a very short time you will quench the Spirit of God in your life. This opens you to all kinds of deception and misery. That is why Scripture plainly teaches that God has ordained all sexual pleasure for the one-flesh marriage relationship.

The Purpose of Dating

Getting to know the person, not the body, is the whole purpose of dating.

When you go out with someone, you learn how they think, discover their personality, observe how they react in good and bad situations and discern their spiritual maturity. Even if you know the person you are dating is the one for you to marry, you should date for a while. When you begin marriage, you do not want to have too many surprises!

The future always must be built upon something which will endure, and temporary things must be built upon things which last. Sex, which is temporary, must be built on relationship, love and marriage, which will last. It cannot happen the other way around.

You will never be successful with your husband or wife physically if you have not first established a good relationship with them. *The relationship between your souls is the foundation for the relationship between your bodies.* The stronger the foundation, the more pleasurable sex will be.

Who and When Not to Marry

Adam might have realized he wanted a wife before he finished naming all the creatures of the earth. Nevertheless, he continued to do what God had called him to do. At the right time, God brought Eve to him. This principle applies to all singles — both men and women — who desire to be married.

If a single person constantly thinks about getting married, they will be frustrated, unhappy and perhaps even unjustly angry at God if it fails to happen within their time frame. With this attitude, they place themselves in a position where they are unable to receive all the blessings the Lord has for them and can hinder the work the Lord has called them to do.

If you desire to be married, put that desire in the Lord's hands and delight and trust in Him. Develop a heart of gratitude. Instead of complaining about what you don't have, form the habit of thanking God for all you do have.

Pleasing God, not looking for a mate, should be the focus of a single person's life.

Following are more scriptural guidelines to help a single person avoid marrying the wrong one. If you are considering marrying someone and know you are going against even one of these principles, God has not brought the right one to you.

1. *Do not marry an unbeliever.* If you are a believer, God is not going to bring you an unbeliever to marry, so don't even date any unbelievers.

> Have we not power to lead about a sister, a wife, as well as other apostles? (1 Corinthians 9:5).

Paul says your wife ought to be your sister in Christ also.

> Be ye not unequally yoked together with unbelievers: for what fellowship hath righteousness with unrighteousness? and what communion hath light with darkness? (2 Corinthians 6:14).

This famous verse needs no explanation.

2. *Do not be in a rush to get married, but let it happen in God's timing.* I encourage teenagers especially to wait to get married until they are older and wiser. The more maturity you have, the better. You are not going to be over the hill if you wait until you are in your twenties. The most important thing at any age is to give yourselves time to be certain you are right for each other, to know one another and to build a strong relationship.

3. *Do not marry in a wave of sexual passion.* Everyone goes through seasons of intense sexual desire. These are not the times to consider getting married. Ride out the wave, and think with your head — not your sexual organs!

4. *Never confuse love with sex — they are not the same.* Sex is an expression of love, not the other way around. Sex only brings fulfillment in a marriage which is already based on the love relationship of two people. Remember, sex is

physical and temporary. It must be built on something enduring, a spiritually based relationship.

5. *Do not marry to solve your problems, or you will exchange one set of problems for another.* Let's say you don't get along with your parents, and you want to get married just to get out of the house. Don't do it! If you seek Him, God will give you the grace to get along with your parents — and eventually perhaps a job so that you can move out!

Do you think you're getting too old? Some of the best marriages come when people are older. It is important to be led by the Holy Spirit and not by your problems — in all areas of your life. Don't marry to escape something. Marry because the Holy Spirit has given you peace about it.

6. *Do not expect marriage to make you happy.* If you are miserable now, chances are you will just bring your spouse into your misery. Find God's will for your life, study His promises and ask the Holy Spirit to instruct you in finding contentment now. Paul wrote that he had *learned* to be content in all things (Philippians 4:11).

Happiness that comes from circumstances is temporary, but happiness which comes from contentment with God is permanent. Once happiness and fulfillment are found, you can look forward to sharing your happiness, not trying to find someone to give happiness to you.

7. *Do not marry a status symbol or an image.* One of the most dangerous things you can do is marry a status symbol, someone who has a lot of money or a good job. Money and social position are not the key ingredients for a good marriage, nor will they in themselves make you happy. Some of the most miserable people are wealthy, famous and influential — even in the Body of Christ.

It would also be a mistake to marry an image — the cheerleader, the football captain or someone you admire because of their looks and popularity.

When I was growing up, the cheerleaders always dated the football players. The rest of us just stood by and sighed, wondering what it would be like to be them. But God planned a great remedy for that kind of thinking when He instituted the ten-year high school reunion. What an eye-opener!

The football captain was bald, and I didn't even recognize the cheerleader because she was so overweight. He drove a truck, and she waited tables. More than that, I found that students who had been "nobodies" in high school were now a bank president, an owner of a chain of restaurants — even a pastor of a great church! So don't marry someone for status or an image. Even they have to grow old and face the realities of life.

8. *Do not marry someone who promises to change after you are married.* If they do not go to church now, don't expect them to go with you after you are married. You want to be certain that whatever changes they make in their life are sincere and lasting. Changes should be made because of their relationship with the Lord, not to manipulate you.

9. *Don't marry someone who is extremely jealous.* Godly jealousy is a good thing. It is a boundary of protection around your marriage relationship. For example, if a man flirted with my wife and she seemed to enjoy it, you can bet I would take her aside and tell her I didn't like it! She would appreciate my jealous reaction, knowing I was protecting her and our marriage.

But extreme jealousy is based on suspicion. Your mate constantly imagines you are cheating on them, so everywhere you go and everything you do is monitored. They don't trust you and probably don't know how to trust anyone. Eventually, jealousy will kill your love.

A biblical example of the destructive nature of jealousy is the account of Saul's jealousy of David. In this case, Saul's unrepented jealousy led to violence and attempted murder. Extreme jealousy is a very dangerous thing.

10. *Finally, do not marry someone who puts you on a*

pedestal or associates you with impossible standards. If a person cannot accept your weaknesses and faults, they cannot accept you. They are looking for someone who is perfect because of some great deficiency in themselves. They are either too lazy or too afraid to deal with their problems, so they look to you instead of God for their sufficiency.

Is God Against Interracial Marriage?

Many people read Scripture passages such as 1 Kings 11:1-3, Exodus 34:16 and Deuteronomy 7:3, where God forbids the children of Israel to marry anyone outside of their own race, and they conclude that God is against interracial marriage. This couldn't be further from the truth.

What God was forbidding was marriage with anyone who did not believe in and worship Him, not with anyone whose skin color was different. He did not want the nation of Israel to mingle with nations who were heathen and who worshipped idols. God allowed marriages when the people of these nations became believers in Him.

With God, the issue has always been a believer not marrying an unbeliever, not races or nationalities.

One excellent example was Rahab, who was a Hittite and a prostitute in Jericho when she came to believe in the God of Israel. When Joshua and the army of Israel approached her city, she hid their spies on the condition that when Israel took the city, she and her family would be spared. Interestingly enough, she is in the genealogy of Jesus.

Another pagan who came to the Lord was Ruth. She was a Moabitess, and the Moabites were bitter enemies of Israel and God. Nevertheless, she also became a believer in the God of Israel and married a Hebrew man named Boaz. Ruth and Boaz were King David's great grandparents and also in the lineage of the Lord Jesus. Others who married foreigners were Joseph, who married an Egyptian, and Moses, who married an Ethiopian.

In choosing a mate, the purity which pleases God has to do with the heart, not the flesh. He is always concerned with our spiritual condition not our physical race.

Still, there are some key issues involved in interracial marriage which should be mentioned. Bringing two races into a marriage can add difficulty. It is hard enough to have a godly, happy home without having to bridge the cultural gap between two races.

I have asked interracial couples, particularly black and white, what their experience has been. Without exception, they have told me that they never understood before they were married the difficulties they would face after they married. Most of these difficulties never go away.

Initial shock, lack of acceptance and prejudice from other people do not cease after a certain number of years. The interracial couple can be viewed as anything from unusual to perverted. What is even harder to bear is that their children face the added challenge of growing up as part of two different groups of people. Often they are accepted by neither. These children can have tremendous identity problems as they try to accept who they are.

Although these problems vary in intensity from one part of the country to another and from one nation to another, they exist everywhere. The couple may think that by moving they will escape the prejudice of others, but there are some people, even in the church, who will never turn from racial prejudice.

The answer to all of the challenges and difficulties of interracial marriage is the same answer to any other problem in life: Jesus Christ. There is nothing the Word of God and the Holy Spirit cannot handle. All of the negative aspects mentioned above can become positive when we turn to those "exceeding great and precious promises."

When our staff counsels an engaged couple who are

from two different races, we ask the same questions we ask all engaged couples: "Are you certain this is God's will for your lives? Do you have complete peace about this?" If they are not absolutely sure this is what God is leading them to do, just like any other couple, we advise them not to marry. Obviously, going against His plan for their lives will only cause heartache, but that heartache is increased in an interracial marriage.

If they have peace from the Holy Spirit about marrying someone from another race, we say go for it! We soberly advise them of the added problems they will face so they will be well prepared and not caught off guard by the enemy. Then we remind them how God's Word and His power will strengthen them and sustain them as they meet every challenge.

When and Whom to Marry

Marry someone because of spiritual things which endure, not because of natural things which are appealing.

You cannot base a marriage on natural things. When I married Loretta, she had a great car, and I love cars. But I'm so glad I didn't marry her for her car, because we sold it two months after we were married!

Your life together must be founded on something more than how you look, what jobs you have, how much money you earn and so forth. Eventually those good looks will fade, you'll retire from your job, and money can only buy so much in life.

> For the Lord seeth not as man seeth; for man looketh on the outward appearance, but the Lord looketh on the heart (1 Samuel 16:7).

Only God can tell you if someone is right for you or not.
You may be dating someone who seems perfect for you,

but your spirit says no. Or you may meet someone who from a natural standpoint does not appeal to you at first, but your spirit says, "That's the one." In any case, the Holy Spirit will make it clear to you whether they are the one, and the sparks will begin to fly — if they haven't already!

I do not believe in "love at first sight," but I do believe Christian couples can know very soon if they are right for each other. Real love and godly passion grow from there. The point to remember is that only the Holy Spirit knows the heart of a person.

The Bible also talks about how the Holy Spirit leads us and guides us — by peace — a supernatural peace which passes all human reason and cannot be denied.

> For ye shall go out with joy, and be led forth with peace (Isaiah 55:12).
> Let us therefore follow after the things which make for peace (Romans 14:19).

You will know you have met the one God has for you because you will have peace about them in your spirit.
You will have a sense of not wanting to live the rest of your life without them. You will realize their life, their calling, their gifts, their personality — *and their faults and weaknesses, which will challenge your faith* — are meant to be a part of your life. (Remember, only Jesus is perfect!)

When your relationship lines up with scriptural principles, and the Holy Spirit bears witness with your spirit that this person is the right one, there is still one more important consideration: What do your trusted friends, parents and elders in the Lord say? If your pastor, parents or mature Christian friends express serious doubts about your marriage, you had better take another look (see Hebrews 13:7,17).

God will always confirm His will for your life through those whom you respect and admire in the faith.

The Focus of Single Life — Setting Priorities

Whether you plan to be married one day or not, one of the most important things you can do while you are single is to set godly priorities. This is the time to establish the habits you want to maintain for the rest of your life. If and when you get married, your mind will be on other things!

The first priority in your life is your relationship with God. Set aside time every day in which He receives your undivided attention. Remember, He gives you His best, twenty-four hours a day, so you can afford to give Him your best, whether it's in the morning, on your lunch hour or before you sleep at night.

When you are single is a time to study God's Word, meditate on His promises and grow close to the Holy Spirit through prayer. Your love for the Lord will grow, and your faith will mature as the Holy Spirit gives you direction for the present and the future. And if you train yourself to spend time with Him as a single, you will bring the daily consistency and stability of that godly habit into your marriage.

Furthermore, maintain an attitude of prayer all day long. This means nothing more than keeping the communication lines open with the Holy Spirit and always being aware of His presence. You might be thanking Him, praising Him, worshipping Him, repenting, seeking wisdom on a matter or asking for the needs and desires of life. This is "praying always with all prayer and supplication" (Ephesians 6:18).

When your spiritual priorities are established, it is easier to get your natural life to line up. Your job, ministry, free time, higher education, social life and so forth become easier to manage when your relationship with God is strong. And it goes without saying that you will find it easier to recognize your mate when he or she comes along if you are in tune with the Spirit of God.

Priorities set early in life make it easier to have a successful marriage. When your life is in order spiritually, you are more likely to be emotionally healthy, mentally strong and stable, and even physically fit. The result is that you will put fewer demands on your future mate to make you happy, and you will be able to give more of yourself to make them happy.

Even if you never marry, setting your priorities and maintaining them will keep you strong in spirit, soul and body. You will be content in all things as Paul was. And, like Paul, you will be free to give to others as the Lord leads you.

Single and Happy — Can It Be?

> But I speak this by permission, and not of commandment. For I would that all men were even as I myself. But every man hath his proper gift of God, one after this manner [single], and another after that [married] (1 Corinthians 7:6-7).

Paul was not just a successful single; he was a happy single! He was so happy being single that he wished everyone was as content. He certainly wasn't saying he wished everybody would remain unmarried, or else the human race would quickly cease to exist! He was saying that it's not being married or staying single that makes you happy; it's your relationship with the Lord that makes you happy.

When Paul says, "I speak this by permission," the word *permission* is a poor translation. This word literally means "concession," or a "joint opinion." Paul is not giving a commandment. He is giving us a joint opinion. He is saying, "This isn't just my opinion, but it is also God's opinion."

He speaks of two gifts in verse 7, the gift of being single and the gift of being married. Both are gifts from God, and neither one is higher or lower than the other. Each gift brings its own way of life and its own set of assets and liabilities. But God has made provision for every situation.

Whether you are married or single, He has already provided all the power, gifts, wisdom and knowledge you need to live a successful life.

If you are called to be single, you will receive the gifts and abilities necessary to be a successful, fulfilled single.

One thing to remember is that being single or married does not change the devil's mode of operation toward you. Just because you have chosen to be single does not mean you will not have temptations, and just because you get married does not mean you won't have to deal with the same temptations.

If singles get their eyes off the Lord, they often begin to feel lonely, yearning for a mate. They think, "If I were married, I wouldn't have to sit alone in church or in restaurants." But when married people get their eyes off the Lord and His promises, they feel lonely, too. A married person can be having dinner with their spouse and children and still feel like something vital is missing from their life.

The married person and the single person may be in the same restaurant, looking at each other, each thinking the other is happy. The grass always looks greener on the other side when you are lonely. But they both have the same problem. They have turned away from the only One who can make them complete.

Both the single person and the married person have forgotten Jesus' promise that He would never leave us or forsake us (Hebrews 13:5). They can do all things through Him (Philippians 4:13), and it is His desire that their joy be full (John 15:11).

If you are feeling lonely, spend some time with Jesus by studying His Word and praying.

This is why it is so important to set priorities. Spending time with the Lord must be number one. Anytime *any* believer feels lonely, empty, frustrated, bored or restless— these are all indications they are not spending enough time in prayer and in God's Word.

Another thing I want to mention to singles has to do with "not forsaking the assembling of ourselves together" (Hebrews 10:25). It is hard to be lonely if you are at church, involved in some area of ministry every time the doors are open. Every member of the congregation should be involved in some way, but singles especially.

All of these things are part of the grace God provides for you in order to live a successful single life.

Jesus Must Be Number One — Always

Jesus tells a story in Luke 14:16-24 about a man who had prepared a great feast and sent his servant out to invite his friends to come join him. The servant returned saying that each of his friends had an excuse for not coming. One had bought a piece of ground he needed to see, another had bought a new team of oxen he had to train, and another had just married and didn't want to leave his wife.

He gives us the bottom line of this story in verse 26:

> If any man come to me, and hate not his father, and mother, and wife, and children, and brethren, and sisters, yea, and his own life also, he cannot be my disciple.

Jesus is not telling us that hating everyone we know is a prerequisite for being His disciple. He is simply saying He must come first in our lives before *and* after we receive natural blessings.

No doubt all these men had been regular guests at this man's table while they were trusting God to help them buy a field, purchase a team of oxen or marry a wife. But like so many believers, they forgot the things of God once their desires were met.

For which of you, intending to build a tower,

158

sitteth not down first, and counteth the cost, whether he have sufficient to finish it? (Luke 14:28).

Taken in the context of the story Jesus has just related, this statement is very profound. Jesus is saying that if you come to the feast of His Word to receive a mate, and then after marriage forsake His Word, you are not counting the cost. A successful marriage requires the spiritual foundation of communion with God and other believers.

If you are single, and your intention is not to establish your relationship with the Lord and the church as a lifelong commitment but merely to "play the game" to receive a mate, you are setting yourself up for a fall. You have not counted the cost.

However, if you decide while you are single that you and your future mate will be regular guests at the Lord's feast, which is the local church, His Word and prayer, then the cost is counted, and a successful marriage can be yours.

But this I say, brethren, the time is short: it remaineth, that both they that have wives be as though they had none (1 Corinthians 7:29).

Paul is saying that the time is getting shorter before the coming of the Lord. If Paul thought the time was short when he wrote this, how much shorter is it today? Even unbelievers sense something incredible is about to take place.

He continues, "It remaineth, that both they that have wives be as though they had none," which does not mean men should ignore their wives. This is another challenge to our priorities. Our relationship with and commitment to the Lord, when married, should be just as important as when we were single.

And they that weep, as though they wept not;

> and they that rejoice, as though they rejoiced not;
> and they that buy, as though they possessed not
> (1 Corinthians 7:30).

Whether you have a good marriage or bad marriage, one that has you rejoicing or weeping, the Lord must remain number one. Whether you have enough money or not, the Lord must be your highest priority in life.

Some believers follow the Lord when they have little prosperity and then forsake Him when finances increase. If they come across financial hard times or marriage problems later, they are back in church seeking counsel.

Priorities should not change because of circumstances or possessions (Philippians 4:11).

When you are single, you should establish a lifelong commitment to the Lord. This season of your life is for learning the Word and communing with the Holy Spirit. Build a strong foundation of study, prayer and godly relationships in church, and they will sustain you in difficult times. Later, if you do marry, this foundation will undergird your marriage.

> And they that use this world, as not abusing it: for the fashion of this world passeth away (1 Corinthians 7:31).

This verse addresses those who are not in full-time ministry but are pursuing a profession in the world instead. As you go out into the world to earn a living, you are to do it legally and ethically. But Paul is also warning you not to lose yourself in your business and forget the Lord.

Getting too involved in a business or profession is a common temptation for singles. Because they do not have a wife and a family to consider, it is easy for them to be distracted from the things of God and church by focusing all their energy and attention on their profession.

Stability and joy are not acquired in your profession or business but in fellowship with the Lord and other believers.

The national economy runs in cycles, Wall Street has its ups and downs, and world markets fluctuate. Moreover, the world is always changing. You can go to college and train for a profession that won't exist ten years from now! However, even though your job may be phased out, Jesus never phases out.

Remember that your business provides finances, not only for you to live, but also to fund the work of the ministry. You are in your profession for two reasons: God has given you the gift to do the work well, and your excellence and stability are a witness to bring your fellow workers to the Lord.

The Giver of the gift or business is the only One you can always rely on, not the gift or the business itself.

> But I would have you without carefulness. He that is unmarried careth for the things that belong to the Lord, how he may please the Lord (1 Corinthians 7:32).

Paul declares to singles, "Don't worry about anything because Jesus is your portion in every area of your life." Whether you have chosen to be single for the present or indefinitely, you will be complete through your relationship with Him. As you desire to please Him, He will fulfill your life.

Paul Chose to Be Single

Most likely, everywhere Paul ministered, couples took him out to eat, leaned over the table and said, "Look, Paul, when are you going to get married?"

Sometimes it is difficult for happily married people to understand how a single person can be complete and fulfilled in Christ, that all the love they would otherwise have showered on a spouse they give back to the Lord, family, friends and those to whom they minister. Single life with Jesus can be just as fulfilling as married life with Jesus.

> Have we not power to lead about a sister, a wife, as well as other apostles, and as the brethren of the Lord, and Cephas? (1 Corinthians 9:5).

I quote this scripture again to emphasize that Paul declared he had the right to take a wife as the other apostles did. However, he chose not to do so, probably because he knew the extent of his calling. He wanted to be able to go when the Lord told him to go without having to consider a wife. With his knowledge of the Word of God and his dedication to living it, I'm sure he would have made a great husband. But his first priority became his all-encompassing passion in life.

> But he that is married careth for the things that are of the world, how he may please his wife (1 Corinthians 7:33).

The greatest advantage of single life is that you have more time for the Lord. What Paul chose to eliminate from his life by not marrying was caring for the things of this world. But notice that the Bible does not say it is a sin to consider the practical, everyday necessities of life. By doing this you are caring for your loved ones.

For example, a husband has to give thought to how he will support his wife and family, where they will live, where they will put the children in school and so forth. In fact, 1 Timothy 5:8 says that if he doesn't do this, he is worse than an unbeliever.

> But if any provide not for his own, and specially

for those of his own house, he hath denied the faith, and is worse than an infidel.

Besides providing for his wife and family, the married man has the desire to please his wife. He wants to make her happy. You can see why being married adds many entanglements, making it more difficult to spend time with the Lord. That is why it is so important to establish a strong relationship with Him when you are single.

In the next verse, Paul talks about the same considerations where a woman is concerned.

> There is difference also between a wife and a virgin. The unmarried woman careth for the things of the Lord, that she may be holy both in body and in spirit: but she that is married careth for the things of the world, how she may please her husband (1 Corinthians 7:34).

The unmarried woman can focus all her attention on pleasing the Lord, growing and maturing in the Word of God, and maintaining her sexual purity as an act of worship to Him. If and when she is married, she will have the added responsibilities of pleasing her husband, running a home and eventually caring for children.

The bottom line of 1 Corinthians 7:29-34 is this: Think before you get married.

Don't jump into marriage without thinking it through, praying about it and having peace from God. Just because you walk in faith doesn't mean you should forget to count the cost and plan for tomorrow. No matter how long you have been single, getting married will change your whole life!

We live in a society of "if it feels good, do it," fast foods, microwave ovens, and instant potatoes. No one has to think. We also live in a society obsessed with sex. Together, these things translate into disastrous marriages.

It is so important for single believers to take advantage of their time alone to establish themselves in the principles of God. Learning to think as God thinks and to do things the way God does them will pay off in times of crises. Then, if they marry and their world turns upside down, this solid foundation in their lives can carry them through.

Finally, Paul says,

> And this I speak for your own profit; not that I may cast a snare upon you, but for that which is comely, and that ye may attend upon the Lord without distraction (1 Corinthians 7:35).

The Holy Spirit has not written all these verses to scare us away from marriage, but to let us know what to expect. Then we won't be distracted by thoughts of, "I wonder what it would be like?" Instead, we can more easily concentrate on the Lord, knowing our time of being single is a special time of maturing.

These verses give all believers a new appreciation for being single. After reading them, we are inspired to let Jesus be the focal point of our lives. However, they are particularly powerful for the single. Like Paul, when a single person embraces the truth and lives their life by it, there will come a day when Philippians 4:11 will describe the condition of their soul also: "I have learned, in whatsoever state I am, therewith to be content."

SEVEN

THE LABOR OF LOVE

We hear it said, the things that come the hardest in life become the most precious to us. As a Christian, I believe this is true. Jesus paid an incredible price for my freedom, trusting I would one day choose to return His love and be His servant and friend. The sacrifice He made to have a relationship with me makes my relationship with Him all the more precious — and the first priority in my life.

But I can say the same thing about my relationship with

Loretta. She is my wife, lover and best friend other than Jesus. Her sacrifices to remain committed to me, love me and care for me — even during times when I cause her pain — do not go unnoticed. The Bible says it best: She is more precious to me than rubies (Proverbs 31:10).

Furthermore, some of the most difficult times in my life are a result of my commitment to Loretta. I too have to make sacrifices and go through changes I would rather avoid. There are times when I grit my teeth, forcing myself to do the right thing or change in order to love her and care for her as the Word commands.

We live in a society today whose moral standard has become, "What is right for me is what is right." The concept of self-sacrifice is equated with losing one's identity or giving up one's destiny. This is completely contrary to scriptural principles, which declare that *personal sacrifice in obedience to God will give you the desires of your heart, not deprive you of them.*

> He that findeth [holds onto] his life shall lose it: and he that loseth his life for my sake shall find it (Matthew 10:39).

Still, there are times when the most spiritual of Christians in the throes of "laying down their lives" for their mates, ask themselves, Is all this worth it? Absolutely! Just as Jesus thought it was worth it to pay the price for a relationship with us, Loretta and I have found it is worth it to pay the price for our marriage. And the blessings that come as a result of our faithfulness and perseverance are far beyond what we could ever imagine. We have truly "found" our lives!

In chapter 1 we looked at Solomon's observation that men who remain faithful to one wife walk in great blessing and prosperity — even if they don't know God ("all the days of thy vanity").

> Live joyfully with the wife whom thou lovest all
> the days of the life of thy vanity, which he hath
> given thee under the sun, all the days of thy
> vanity: for that is thy portion in this life, and in
> thy labour which thou takest under the sun (Ec-
> clesiastes 9:9).

The last phrase of this verse is the subject of this chapter,
"thy labour which thou takest under the sun." This is giving
us the cold hard fact that a good marriage is available to
everyone, but it takes work.

*To enter into the blessings of marriage, you are going to
have to do some hard labor!*

The Corinthian Challenge

No group of people came to understand this principle
more than the Corinthians. At the time the Gospel came to
Corinth, it was the Las Vegas of its time. Everything was
legal, and sexual sin was the accepted way of life.

Corinth was also one of the most intellectual cities of
ancient Greece. Historically, cities and nations that focus
on the human mind without knowledge of spiritual truth
are also immersed in gross immorality.

Not only was prostitution legal in Corinth, it was part of
the people's worship to the Greek gods. People worshipped Venus, the goddess of love, by having sex with the
priests and priestesses in the temple which honored her.
The common belief in Corinth was that sex for pleasure
was accomplished outside of marriage. The only time you
had sex with your spouse was to have children.

Moreover, Corinth was divided into tribes, and it was
traditional to keep the tribes pure and separate from one
another. Marriages were arranged by the parents in the
tribe long before the children were grown. It was strictly
forbidden to have children outside of the marriage contract.

Young people were not consulted in choosing their mates, nor did they have much contact with them after they were married. It was the wife's job to bear children and keep the household running, while the husband went about his business. They had sex only to have children. The rest of the time they would each go to the temple for sexual gratification. Also, because homosexuality was legal and very common, many of the men and women practiced this at the temple.

Nearly every principle of God's Word defied the pagan religion of Corinth. So Paul had the task of laying a foundation in the basics of morality, doctrine and church etiquette as he wrote the Book of First Corinthians.

The Corinthians didn't believe in resurrection, so he addressed the necessity and power of Jesus' resurrection in 1 Corinthians 15. They abused spiritual gifts so badly, he took three chapters (12-14) to teach on the simplicity of the operation of spiritual gifts. They didn't understand communion, turning it into a wild, drunken party, so in chapter 11 Paul instructed them in the sacredness of that rite.

After Paul left Corinth, the new believers found out God did not want them to have sex outside of marriage. They learned that the husband and wife were meant for each other's sexual pleasure as well as for the birth of children. The whole idea of being faithful to your spouse was totally foreign to their previous way of life and thinking.

They were so upset they sent Paul a letter, asking him to clear up the issue. So Paul wrote them about sex and marriage:

> Now concerning the things whereof ye wrote unto me: It is good for a man not to touch a woman. Nevertheless, to avoid fornication, let every man have his own wife, and let every woman have her own husband (1 Corinthians 7:1-2).

Because anything pleasurable was legal in Corinth, these simple statements written by Paul were shocking to the new converts there. Like many new Christians, they had to be taught what God declares to be sin. In their ignorance, they brought sexual perversion into the church.

In the first verse Paul tells them they should not have sex either before or outside of marriage. The singles began to cry, "You mean I've got to wait until I'm married to have sex?" In verse 2 he goes on to say that God ordained one man for one woman, and sex is for pleasure only within the confines of marriage. No doubt the married people in the congregation dropped their jaws and turned to take long, hard looks at their spouses! Their whole way of life was being turned around.

There were probably many believers in Corinth who were married to unbelieving spouses, promiscuous spouses or homosexuals. Even worse, many new converts had been accustomed to operating in sexual sin themselves. Every possible reason for divorce existed. Nevertheless, Paul declared to them, "God can work it out."

Grace for the Impossible

Often a couple will walk into my office for pre-marriage counseling and announce that God has brought them together. They glowingly declare how they are perfect for one another and will never have any problems. I know immediately they may know how to *find* the right one, but they know nothing about *living* with the right one.

God unites hearts together in marriage. In the spirit you are complete, and it's wonderful. But the joining of the flesh is what's difficult! I'm not just referring to sex, but the little things in the natural that a husband and wife encounter in their daily lives together. These are insignificant things which can become major issues, ultimately affecting their sexual relationship.

For example, I have often wondered if all women squeeze the toothpaste tube from the middle. I was taught, most efficiently, to squeeze it from the bottom and roll it up, but Loretta would grab the middle and mess up my work of art! How did we finally solve this problem? Did I convert her to my way of thinking? Did I eventually loosen up and learn to tolerate her way of handling the tube? No — we bought two tubes of toothpaste.

And let's not forget the rude awakening the morning after the first night of the honeymoon. Her makeup is not only smeared on her face but all over his pillow. He leans over and affectionately says hi, and she winces with disgust at his breath.

When the honeymoon is over, he discovers she doesn't bake biscuits the way his mother did. In fact, she doesn't cook anything the way he likes it. Her neat, orderly world is shattered as she discovers whiskers in the sink, the toilet seat always left up and his underwear all over the bedroom floor. After all, mother always picked up after him!

Few marriages break up over something monumental. Rather, they are sunk by the little things which mount up day after day, festering until they become major problems. But these problems are nothing compared to the Corinthians'. If they could have happy marriages, yours is a cinch!

Undaunted, Paul moves to the heart of the matter — what the King James Version calls "due benevolence."

> Let the husband render unto the wife due benevolence: and likewise also the wife unto the husband (1 Corinthians 7:3).

The word *render* means to give, but the word *due* indicates this is something they *owe one another*. *Render* means you have the choice to give it, but *due* means you are obligated by God to give it.

For example, my church staff members are called by God to their positions, and they all approach their ministry as unto the Lord. But on the first and fifteenth of every month, they expect their paychecks! Twice a month I *decide* to give them what I *owe* them. In the same way, your husband or wife can expect you to give them "benevolence."

The word *benevolence* often brings to mind a charitable donation to the poor. But it is translated from one of the most beautiful Greek words, *eunoia*, a compound word. *Eu* means "good," and *noia* means "mind." This does not mean you give your spouse a good piece of your mind!

Eunoia means you owe it to your spouse to think about them in goodness and grace. You owe them "grace thinking." The extra courtesy given during courtship does not end at marriage. What is owed in marriage is not primarily sex but *consideration*. Loving thoughts and kind affection are *due* each other.

Men, if you want to be more successful with your wife in bed, quit pawing her when you come home from work and talk to her instead. Sex is more than a means of working off the stress of a hard day. Sex is for *two*. Give your wife some kind words and attention — ask about her stressful day. Listen affectionately about the children, her friends or her job outside the home. You *owe* her this. Then see if your lovemaking doesn't take a turn for the better!

Wives, don't jump all over your husband when he comes home and expect him to get right into your flow of things. Find out how he best makes the transition from being at work to being at home, and let him ease into it. Prepare yourself to meet him with love and understanding, and see if he doesn't treat you better for your consideration.

Benevolence, or grace thinking, is taking the attitude toward your mate that God takes toward you.

God's love is unconditional, and He is long-suffering toward you. Instead of badgering your mate about their faults, consider your own. Does God provoke you over your faults? No, God treats you the way you used to treat each other when you dated. Courtship and courtesy should never end when the marriage begins. Their rewards are too valuable to neglect.

Men are not great lovers because of their broad shoulders, strong muscles, wavy hair or great car. Inner strength and a servant's heart are more desirable to a wise woman than outward strength or financial means. Nor is a woman a great lover because of her fantastic figure and beautiful face. Inner beauty and a kind heart are more desirable to a mature man than an attractive outward appearance.

I've seen a man drop a good-looking wife for a woman who wasn't as pretty simply because the wife never made him feel he was worthy of her. The "other woman" treated him with respect and practiced grace thinking. I've also seen a woman leave a macho husband with a tan and muscles for a man who was bald and had big ears. She went for a man who gave her kindness and made her a first priority in his life, leaving her "hunk" of a husband scratching his head.

Looks will fade, but an attitude of grace will endure and sustain a relationship.

During the time you dated, you won each other's thoughts and hearts. You were trying to out-give and out-love each other. Now that you are married, you owe each other the same consideration. It is not God's will for you to get married, become insensitive and give no thought to the other person.

Love is a mental attitude.

One of the most important aspects of grace thinking is this: Even if your mate hasn't pleased you, you want to please them. Grace doesn't say, "I'll please you if you please me." Grace says, "I'll please you whether you please me or not." When both the husband and the wife have this attitude, the marriage relationship becomes more fun every day.

Just How Often Should We Have Sex?

This is usually the question the wife asks! But I'm sure the Corinthians, as they desperately tried to sort out their new lives in Christ sexually, were also interested to know this.

> The wife hath not power of her own body, but the husband: and likewise also the husband hath not power of his own body, but the wife. Defraud ye not one the other, except it be with consent for a time, that ye may give yourselves to fasting and prayer; and come together again, that Satan tempt you not for your incontinency (1 Corinthians 7:4-5).

Your body belongs to your mate, and your mate's body belongs to you. The wife actually possesses her husband's body, and he possesses hers. Like your relationship with Jesus, you are no longer your own. In marriage, you belong to your spouse. However, this is only successful if you are both giving toward each other, thinking with grace.

Don't expect the blessings of God to fill your life if you are quoting Scripture to use your spouse selfishly for sex.

Paul's language in verse 5 is very strong. Another translation says, "Stop depriving one another!" (NAS). Unless there is a legitimate reason, you should not even think about saying no if your husband or wife desires you sexually. The only time you would abstain from sex is when you mutually consent to pray for a time ("fasting" is not in the Greek text).

This verse shows how important sex is in the marriage relationship. Married couples should experience physical intimacy frequently. God commands this because it keeps your relationship healthy and strong. One of the signs that your priorities are falling out of line or that trouble has crept into your relationship is a lack of sexual intimacy and pleasure in sex.

Again we can see a parallel to your relationship with the Lord. When your priorities are in line and you are keeping your heart pure before Him, you have no problem worshipping Him face-to-face. But when your life is out of balance or you have given place to sin, it is hard to look Jesus in the eye and tell Him that you love Him.

In the same way, complete joy and pleasure in loving your mate sexually is the result of practicing grace thinking. If you are holding something against your spouse, or if strife and division have come between you, it will be difficult to make love to them face to face. Only when you choose to have an attitude of forgiveness and compassion will you again fully enjoy making love to your spouse. Having sex is a time of affirming your love and trust.

Intimately praising and worshipping the Lord brings strength and stability to your life and acts as a safeguard to keep you on the right path. Likewise, the intimacy of making love with your spouse brings strength and stability into your marriage and is a key factor in keeping your relationship on the right track.

The Underestimated Power of Prayer

One of the most important keys to a good marriage is also found in 1 Corinthians 7:5: *prayer*. First, the verse tells us there should be "consent" in abstaining from sexual relations for a time. "Consent" implies communication and agreement.

Next, consider *why* you would agree to abstain. A couple may have set aside time to pray about a family crisis, a pressing need in their church, a marriage problem or a need for direction.

When your marriage has a problem or you are facing a difficult decision, make prayer together your first step. Stop everything in the natural and surrender yourselves to the supernatural wisdom and power of God. The best Counselor is the Holy Spirit, and He has the answer to whatever situation or conflict you are facing.

If an issue has become so volatile between you that you can't pray together, see a church counselor. Unfortunately, many Christians come for counseling to find someone who will agree with them against their mate. They are not really interested in changing themselves, but only their spouse. However, if they come to learn — not to argue their case — their marriage can grow.

If husbands and wives would pray together for fifteen to thirty minutes every day, hand-in-hand, taking every concern and dispute to the Lord and asking for His wisdom, I guarantee God would answer them and meet whatever need they had. Praying together is one of the keys to a successful, fulfilling marriage.

This Scripture verse stresses that one of the most subtle ways a marriage can begin to have problems is by slowly moving away from the priority of prayer. Couples often change their priorities after they are married. Don't fall into this trap! When you get married, you add a new responsibility to your life, but your spiritual priorities must remain the same.

As a couple, set aside a time to study the Bible together — especially passages of Scripture that address the marriage. I recommend studying 1 Corinthians 13 from the Amplified Bible. Any married couple who dedicates themselves to living this chapter can have a tremendous marriage.

Problem Solving

When marriage problems arise, I have learned several things that help solve them.

First, magnify your faults and weaknesses, not your

mate's. We all tend to minimize and justify our own faults, but blow our mate's faults out of proportion. By looking at our own faults and dealing with them, not only can we avoid strife with our mate, but also we will grow up. You cannot change yourself without crucifying your flesh! And when you form the habit of pointing the finger at yourself instead of your spouse, you will have a lot more compassion and patience for your partner.

Second, practice listening instead of talking — and the word "practice" is the key. Listening is a skill you acquire by practicing it. Have you ever tried to tell someone something, but they interrupt you before you end your sentence? Then what they say indicates they didn't hear a word you just said? We all do this from time to time because we haven't learned the art of listening.

These first two points were difficult for me personally. When Loretta and I were considering divorce and then recommitted ourselves to working out our marriage, I thought it would turn around in a week. But after a couple of months, we were still having immense problems. Most of them had to do with poor communication and pride. I wanted her to hear and understand my side, and she wanted me to hear and understand her side.

Finally I asked her to tell me again what her complaints were, and I made the supreme effort to write them down. I expected to be writing for several hours. Based on all the times she had talked to me about them, I was certain there must be at least one hundred. To my surprise there were only seven or eight.

You see, I had not been listening to her. Whenever she started to tell me anything, I just assumed she was rattling off my many faults, and I would tune her out.

This time as she said each one, I felt like throwing something at her, but I managed to control my temper and get them on paper. When she finished, she said, "I'm not saying you're filled with faults. It's just that some of them are canceling out your good points."

I took my list with me when I went on my next speaking engagement. While I was away, I prayed, asking the Lord to show me if she was right or wrong. I said, "Lord, if she's wrong, I want to approach her in love. Show me how You want me to set her straight."

The Lord interrupted my unselfish prayer and said, "Guess what? All of them are right!" It took a day and a half for Him to convince me. On the first day, He showed me everything she had said. During the next half-day, I tried to argue Him out of it. Only when I finally realized all this was from God did I call Loretta and tell her.

That phone call brought one of the greatest breakthroughs in our marriage. The strongholds of poor communication and self-centeredness were being exposed. Slowly but surely they were replaced with habits of good communication and honesty.

When you are able to strip away pride, see yourself exactly as you are and admit to your facades, fears and weaknesses, then your mate can begin to relate to you.

As I opened myself up to Loretta and came to terms with my shortcomings, she began to open up to me. After baring my soul to her, she could trust me enough to discuss her own faults, fears and weaknesses. For the first time in a long time, we were really talking and listening to one another. Our friendship was operating again.

Third, once the problem has been clearly stated and understood, discuss solutions and answers. Mark 11:24 does not say, "What things soever are your problems." If you dwell on the problem, you will keep hurt and confusion alive and even stir up more problems. In that atmosphere the Holy Spirit cannot communicate any answers to you. Pray your "desires," the answers to your problems.

God knows the problem, so you don't need to keep bringing it up. What you need to pray is the answer, which is His will for your lives. Working toward solutions instead of dwelling on problems brings your faith alive to receive the grace you need. Then you can overcome all situations.

Finally, remember that love is not a feeling; it is a choice. The Bible says faith works by love, but we could turn that around and say love works by faith, too. There are times when you have to choose to love your mate and trust the feelings to come later.

You will have moments when you grit your teeth, push an encouraging word out of your mouth and force yourself to be affectionate. But the rewards of doing right are always great. Because you are basing your actions on God's Word and not your feelings, I guarantee it won't be long before the spark of love will be there again!

There is a supernatural law in the Bible which says that as a man thinks in his heart, so is he (Proverbs 23:7), that whatever you choose to believe in your heart will determine the course of your life (Mark 11:23-24). It may take some time to manifest in the natural, but the moment you set your heart and mind to believe it, it begins to take form in your life.

> And beyond all these things put on love, which is
> the perfect bond of unity (Colossians 3:14, NAS).

When you set your heart and mind to choose to love your husband or wife, which is in line with God's Word, there will come a time when you love your mate passionately. In fact, because your love is based on the grace of God and not your own strength, you will love your spouse more than you ever dreamed possible.

In-Laws

While we are on the subject of conflict and problems in marriage, let's look at a passage of Scripture that addresses the issue of in-laws.

Therefore shall a man shall leave his father and his mother, and shall cleave unto his wife: and they shall be one flesh (Genesis 2:24).

Leaving in-laws was commanded before in-laws ever existed!

Cutting the apron strings is vital to the success of any marriage. One of the major causes for divorce are meddling in-laws who cannot stay out of their children's affairs, and children who marry and refuse to grow up and take responsibility for their own lives. They are constantly running home to Mom or Dad whenever any challenge, discomfort or pain occurs, instead of coming together with their spouse and seeking the wisdom and strength from God to work things out.

The word *leave* used here does not mean you never see your mother and father again; it means "to leave the authority of your parents." As soon as you are married, your parents no longer have authority in your life. You will always *honor* them (Exodus 20:12; Ephesians 6:2), which is an attitude of respect and gratitude. However, you no longer look to them as you did when you were growing up. You become one flesh with your spouse, and you accept that your primary counselor is no longer your father or mother but your husband or wife.

Many parents say, "Well, I'm just trying to help them avoid making mistakes." Let them make their own mistakes! That is one of the ways people grow up, and sometimes they learn the most valuable lessons through their mistakes. Or they say, "Well, we don't want them to make the same mistakes we made." That's the value of training them up in the way they should go (Proverbs 22:6).

While you're training them, and when they are old enough, tell them about your mistakes. Let them know how you suffered for disobeying God here or for rebelling against God there. Then when they are married, trust the

ONE FLESH

truth you've put into them and cut the strings. Be available only if they really need you.

When parents and children clearly cut the ties and fully recognize the new marriage, in-laws can be a wonderful blessing. The parents of a married couple can be a great support and source of wisdom to them through the years.

The Power of Sanctification

In 1 Corinthians 7:10 Paul addressed those marriages in which both partners were believers. Now in verse 12 he begins to talk to believers who are married to unbelievers. He refers to them as "the rest."

> But to the rest speak I, not the Lord: If any brother hath a wife that believeth not, and she be pleased to dwell with him, let him not put her away. And the woman which hath an husband that believeth not, and if he be pleased to dwell with her, let her not leave him (1 Corinthians 7:12-13).

There are two ways in which you can be unequally yoked in marriage. Either you have married an unbeliever against the Word of God, or you have become born again after you were married. In either case, what are you supposed to do when you, a believer, are married to an unbeliever? Paul says if you are married to an unbeliever, and he or she still loves you and wants to live with you, you should not divorce that person.

Just because your mate is an unbeliever does not give you grounds for divorce.

Notice Paul says, "But to the rest speak I, not the Lord." The reason he qualifies his statement is because Jesus never taught about marriage between a believer and an unbeliever in His public ministry. Therefore, Paul had to seek wisdom from the Holy Spirit for this situation.

Under the New Testament, if you are married when you receive Jesus, and your spouse rejects the Lord but does not reject you, you are to remain married to them. It is amazing to me how someone can receive Jesus as their Lord and Savior and then want to divorce their unbelieving mate, dissolving all vows to them. If God had you break all vows made prior to salvation, you wouldn't pay your bills or go to work either.

Knowing Jesus Christ ought to make you want to strengthen those vows not abandon them. Even more, knowing Him should also give you the desire to see your mate saved. Divorcing them is not exactly a great witness!

Before we go on with this passage of Scripture, I want to bring in some verses from Matthew 5 which speak of how we are to be salt and light before unbelievers.

> Ye are the salt of the earth: but if the salt have lost his savor, wherewith shall it be salted? it is thenceforth good for nothing, but to be cast out, and to be trodden under foot of men (Matthew 5:13).

When Jesus says we are the salt of the *earth,* He means the literal ground on which we stand. Everywhere we go, we are the salt for that place.

Salt does three things: it preserves, it flavors, and it hinders. In Jesus' time, before there was refrigeration, meat was salted to *preserve* it. And we know the value of the *flavor* of salt. Can you imagine eating foods such as egg whites or grits without salt? Then there's the *hindering* aspect of salt. In the ancient world, conquering armies would throw salt in a field and plow it into the ground to keep anything from growing there.

The same salt that preserves and flavors can also hinder, and this refers to a believer's authority over the works of

Satan. The same believer who can cause blessing and long life to come to those for whom they pray can also stop the forces of the enemy against them.

Your presence brings blessing, flavor and protection into your home. These characteristics are in sharp contrast to the joyless, bland and dangerous world we live in. Why has our country been so blessed? Because we have a great presence of salt!

> Ye are the light of the world. A city that is set on an hill cannot be hid. Neither do men light a candle, and put it under a bushel, but on a candlestick; and it giveth light unto all that are in the house. Let your light so shine before men, that they may see your good works, and glorify your Father which is in heaven (Matthew 5:14-16).

You are not only the salt of the *earth,* but you are the light of the *world.* These words are translated differently because they are different Greek words. Where the "earth" in verse 13 means the physical ground we stand on, the "world" in verse 14 means the *kosmos,* or the world system. We are the light in a dark, Satan-dominated world.

Putting your light under a bushel is the same as salt losing its savor — neither one is good for anything. So we are to be the light of this world, first in the house and then before all men. As I related earlier, I came to understand this reality deeply in my own life: *Your light won't shine any brighter in the world than it does in your own home.*

Many believers are zealous to be witnesses in the world — to be salt and light on the job, at their fitness center and in their neighborhood. But in their own families they quit at the first sign of trouble. They are willing to trust God for healing of diseases, restoration of financial losses and resolution of problems on the job, but they have no desire to see their marriages healed and restored, especially when they are married to unbelieving mates.

But 1 Corinthians 7:12-13 establishes that when the unbeliever is pleased to dwell with the believer, there are no grounds for divorce. The unbelieving spouse is committed to you, willing to work out any problems that arise, even though they have not received Jesus.

Imagine a man and woman being married when they are unbelievers. Everything is great, until one day the wife comes home and says, "Honey, I don't know how to tell you this, but I went to church with my friend Mildred this Sunday. Well, everything there was very different. The pastor gave his sermon, and my heart was really touched. When he asked if anyone wanted to receive Jesus as their Lord and Savior, I just knew he was talking to me. So I went to the front and, well, I was born again!"

"What does that mean," he asks in disbelief.

"Well, it means I'm a Christian. I mean, I can really talk to God now, and He talks to me, because I'm His child."

"Sounds to me like you've been brainwashed!"

"No! Come on, honey, I wasn't at the church long enough to be brainwashed. Honestly, this is a good thing for us, not a bad thing."

"All right, I just want to know one thing. How is this going to affect our marriage? Are you going to preach at me all the time and nag me about going to this church?"

"No. I hope that our marriage will be better. I won't lie to you and say I don't care if you don't go to church or get saved, but I know Jesus will help me to be a better wife. Already, I feel more love for you than I ever have."

So this man is still pleased to dwell with his wife, even though she is a believer. As a result, some very interesting things begin to happen in his life, because his wife "has gotten religion!"

For the first time in their married life, she begins to be careful about the money she spends, sticking to the budget they have agreed upon. Of course, she asks him if she can give a certain amount of their income each month, telling she believes God will bless him in his job. He says he'll try it for three months. To his amazement, he receives a promotion and a raise!

Then he realizes the house looks nicer than ever before, meals are fixed better, but she doesn't look more tired. In fact, she looks better than ever—and sex is great! The only thing she insists upon is that time of prayer and reading her Bible in the morning, and going to church on Sunday and midweek. He is especially baffled by the fact that whenever any of the family gets sick, she begins to pray scriptures from the Bible, and they seem to get well faster!

Whether he realizes it or not, this husband is living the life of a sanctified mate.

Jesus declared that the Holy Spirit would give us power to be witnesses (Acts 1:8), and some of the greatest witnesses are believers who are married to unbelievers. The great English evangelist Smith Wigglesworth was saved because of the love and faith of his wife. Although he had forbidden her to go to church, she went anyway. One night when she returned from a service, she found the door to the house locked. Mrs. Wigglesworth just curled up by the front door and slept there.

When Smith opened the door to get the paper the next morning, she jumped up, gave him a kiss and said, "Good morning, Smith. What can I fix you for breakfast?" This act of unconditional love broke his hardened heart, and he received Jesus as his Lord. He went on to cross the globe preaching the gospel, and not only were thousands saved, but incredible miracles were done through his ministry.

Not all spouses are saved as quickly as Smith Wigglesworth, and some spouses never receive the Lord. But as long as the unbeliever is pleased to dwell with the believing mate, the believer should stay married, committed to be the best husband or wife they can be. Through the believer's faithfulness, their mate is sanctified, or receives special blessing from the Lord. In many cases the unbelieving spouse gets saved.

> For the unbelieving husband is sanctified by the wife, and the unbelieving wife is sanctified by the husband: else were your children unclean; but now are they holy (1 Corinthians 7:14).

What will happen to the children who are raised in a spiritually divided home? The believer is probably worried about whether or not the children will receive the Lord — and so is the unbelieving spouse! Who will win the hearts of those children? Who is more influential?

This verse of Scripture says the believer is the powerful one in the marriage because he or she sanctifies the mate and the children. This does not mean that because you are born again, your mate is too. However, because you are saved, you bring special blessings and favor from God to him or her. It's a spiritual principle — you are salt and light in your house.

Through your prayers, you surround your family with a hedge of protection. Your children observe how your faith adds love, peace and joy to the home. They see how you bring favor to their other parent in their work and to them in school. You shine the light of God's wisdom into the home, and problems that seemed insurmountable become solvable.

The Bible says the believer is the dominant spiritual force in the home. Because of the believer's presence, God sees the children as holy. Consequently, He works at all times to bring success to the children through the believing parent's prayers and witness. When the time comes for them to choose, the children will be inclined to choose Jesus instead of the world. Light is always stronger than darkness.

The Stripes of Jesus

In a spiritually divided household, the only way you can maintain your personal holiness and keep your household sanctified is through daily study of God's Word. Colossians 4:6 says we are to season all our words with salt, which is the Word. This doesn't mean every time you open your mouth you preach Scripture at them, but everything you say should be a reflection of the truth inside you.

In addition, you also keep yourself sanctified by living the Word of God, not just studying it. If your mate gives you a hard time because you go to church, instead of letting them have it, remember that "a soft answer turneth away wrath" (Proverbs 15:1). Show your partner love and respect. Love is the most powerful witness to an unbelieving mate and unbelieving children.

> But as God hath distributed to every man, as the Lord hath called every one, so let him walk. And so ordain I in all churches (1 Corinthians 7:17).

No matter what our situation may be, God has distributed sufficient grace for us to handle it.

When I married my wife, God gave me the grace to live with her and make her happy. He gave her the grace to live with me and make me happy. In the beginning we failed to use His grace. We had to change ourselves to line up with His Word and appropriate His grace.

If you were born again after you were married, and your spouse does not want to receive Jesus, then you too have been given sufficient grace to live with them if they are pleased to dwell with you. You accomplish this by abiding in the Word of God.

We are all tempted to compare our mates with someone else. The Bible says comparing ourselves with each other is not wise (2 Corinthians 10:12). My paraphrase of 1 Corinthians 7:17 is, "Quit griping about your position in life and walk in the grace God has given you. Watch His power bring a miracle in your marriage!"

If your mate insults you because of your faith, it doesn't necessarily mean they are not pleased to dwell with you. They may be under incredible conviction by the Holy Spirit because of your prayers and witness. (This situation also can exist between Christian couples when one partner is out of fellowship with the Lord.) Remember: *God has called you in the midst of suffering to appropriate His grace and receive victory.*

> For even hereunto were ye called: because Christ also suffered for us, leaving us an example, that ye should follow his steps: Who did no sin, neither was guile found in his mouth: Who, when he was reviled, reviled not again; when he suffered, he threatened not; but committed himself to him that judgeth righteously: Who his own self bare our sins in his own body on the tree, that we, being dead to sins, should live unto righteousness: by whose stripes ye were healed (1 Peter 2:21-24).

Jesus suffered because He was right, not because He was wrong. His attitude toward and His reaction to suffering for the gospel is our example today. Whenever He went through persecution, He did not return evil for evil but forgave and turned the situation over to the Father. He was a blessing to those around Him, and He always emerged the conqueror.

When your mate is reviling you for the gospel's sake, your tendency in the flesh is to rise up and criticize them, to cut them down. But when you do that, you are taking judgment out of God's hands and putting it into your own hands. Leave it in God's hands! He is the perfect Judge over all situations. Besides, if Jesus did it, it must be the best thing to do!

Verse 24 says, "that we, being dead to sins." Declare that you are dead to the sin of criticism! Establish in your heart and mind that criticism will not bother you anymore. If you make this commitment and stick with it, you will be free and victorious in the midst of harassment. This is one of the greatest witnesses to the unbeliever or the spouse who is out of fellowship with the Lord.

Peter goes on to say, "by whose stripes we were healed." We usually use this phrase with regard to physical healing. That's correct, but in the context of this chapter we have limited the scope of this verse.

According to Deuteronomy 25:1-3, if a controversy arose between two men, it was to be taken to the judges, who would decide who was right and who was wrong in the matter. The wicked one would then be given the appropriate number of lashes, not to exceed forty, which was the maximum — the same number of stripes Jesus took for our healing.

In 1 Peter 2:24, Peter is quoting Isaiah 53:5:

> But he was wounded for our transgressions, he was bruised for our iniquities: the chastisement of our peace was upon him; and with his stripes we are healed.

The stripes of Jesus bring physical healing as well as peace to our lives.

What scripture can you trust for the healing of your home life? "By whose stripes ye were healed!" As sure as He bore those stripes for cancer and tuberculosis, He bore them so we might have peace in the midst of the storm. We can stand confidently, knowing He will cause peace to triumph over any controversy.

A Word About Incompatibility

There should be no such thing as incompatibility in marriage between two born-again believers. There was a time when my wife and I swore we had no love for each other — none. She said to me, "I don't love you. In fact, I believe I married the wrong person." Then I started to think that maybe I had married the wrong person, too. Remember, we were going in two different directions.

Nevertheless, we discovered that our feelings and our own feeble understanding did not amount to anything when we stepped out in faith and chose to love one another again. Like the believer who is diagnosed with a disease and chooses to believe he is healed by the stripes of Jesus, Loretta and I chose to believe we loved one another.

We forced ourselves to think and speak as if we cared for one another, liked each other and were meant for each other. We prayed God's Word over our marriage: "Thank you, Father. Your unconditional love is shed abroad in our hearts, and we love one another." Instead of focusing on the other person's faults, we thanked God for their strengths and good character.

This begins as hard work, but eventually it becomes easier. You start to notice how your feelings are falling in line with what you are choosing to believe, pray and act upon.

One day when you walk in the door after a hard day at work, it hits you that you can't wait to put your arms around your wife. You don't have to force yourself anymore! Finally it dawns on you that love is not a feeling but a choice — a commitment.

The deeper feelings of passion and trust are a pleasant result of the daily choices to love the right one.

Today my love for Loretta is greater than I ever could have imagined when I made the decision to love her years ago in that hotel room. One word of caution, though. We still have days when we don't feel as if we love each other. Now, however, we do not allow the lack of emotion to rule our hearts and minds. As we choose to live according to God's Word and not according to our feelings, our relationship grows and becomes stronger.

There is something much more powerful than any problem you face in your life, including marriage problems, and that is the Word of God. There was a day when I thought our marriage was an absolute impossibility. I thought I found one situation and one person God couldn't change, but I was wrong. When we finally made the decision to work out our problems, find out what God's Word had to say and release His promises into our marriage, our whole relationship turned around.

The Greatest Investment

And in thy labour which thou takest under the sun (Ecclesiastes 9:9).

Marriage is work! Those unbelievers who have good marriages have accepted this fact and have chosen to work at their marriages. They have discovered that it is extremely rewarding work. If Christians work at their marriages, God will work right along with them, and the rewards are even more tremendous.

Again, it is incredible to me how much time a husband will spend pursuing a hobby, investing so much of his money, time and effort in something that will give him very little return in this life — and none eternally.

Businessmen and businesswomen will contribute most of their energy and thinking toward their professions, working long hours during the week and on weekends, letting their mates become strangers to them. Many homemakers get caught up in hobbies or organizations —

even in the church — which can distract them from spending time with their husbands. One day that man will retire, and you need to consider, "What will we talk about? What will we do together? How will our lives fit together?"

God has designed something which gives you a manifold return for the amount of work you invest in it: your marriage. As you contribute to your marriage, spend time with your spouse, help them and work with them, the blessings are multiplied. In later years the marriage just gets better and better.

> Though our outward man perish, yet the inward man is renewed day by day (2 Corinthians 4:16).

Applying this verse to your marriage will cause your love to grow stronger each day no matter what problems or obstacles you face. It is impossible for you to imagine the blessings that will come into your life through the time, effort and sacrifice you put into your marriage. As you grow old together, every good seed you have planted in each other's lives will multiply back to you in joy and fulfillment — far beyond your wildest dreams! 🍂

EIGHT

GOD HAS CALLED YOU TO PEACE

If a mass murderer on death row got saved and was miraculously released from prison, most churches today would beg him to come and give his testimony and preach the gospel. On the other hand, many full-time ministers who have given years of service to the Lord are shunned by factions of the body of Christ because they have been divorced or because they have been divorced and remarried.

Until recent years, it seemed that the unpardonable sin

was not the sin of rejecting Jesus Christ as Lord and Savior, but rather divorce. The Church has been notorious for doing everything from excommunicating divorced people to subtly snubbing them in local church fellowship. Today churches have had to stop shunning divorced people purely because there are almost as many divorces among Christians as among non-Christians. Some churches would lose half their congregation if they disallowed them!

Don't misunderstand. I am not minimizing the sin of divorce, but let's put it into biblical perspective. The following passage of Scripture lists the seven things God hates, and you will notice that divorce is not among them.

> These six things doth the Lord hate: yea, seven are an abomination unto him: A proud look, a lying tongue, and hands that shed innocent blood, an heart that deviseth wicked imaginations, feet that be swift in running to mischief, a false witness that speaketh lies, and he that soweth discord among brethren (Proverbs 6:16-19).

God hates all types of sin, and there is no question He hates divorce. His Word declares it in Malachi 2:16. We can understand why He hates divorce so passionately after studying His design for marriage, which is a type of our relationship with Him. Divorcing my mate is a type of turning my face away from the Lord.

Nevertheless, divorce is not the unpardonable sin.

Just as God hates sin but loves the sinner, He hates divorce but loves the divorced person. There is still a place in the Body of Christ for you if you have been divorced. You can be fully restored to that place — no matter what the office or position — if you come to terms with your divorce. You must allow the Holy Spirit to change the things in your life which caused it and heal the wounds that are a result of it.

Is There Scriptural Divorce?

This is the first question most divorcing individuals must face, but most have no idea if there is such a thing as "scriptural divorce." Although the Bible gives several allowances for divorce, it states that the root cause for all divorces is hardness of heart. Jesus spoke of this in Matthew 19:8 when He said it was because of the people's hardness of heart that God allowed Moses to institute the writ of divorce.

When one or both of the marriage partners hardens their hearts against their mates, they are hardening their hearts against God. Some may harden their hearts against God and then turn against their mates. In either case, if they do not repent and turn back to the Lord and be reconciled with their spouses, they will eventually divorce.

One of the worst manifestations of hardness of heart, which is also scriptural grounds for divorce, is physical abuse. Spouse beating has become epidemic in the world, but it is almost as prevalent in the church. It is ironic that the key verse dealing with physical abuse is Malachi 2:16.

Most Christians read the first part of Malachi 2:16, which says God hates divorce, and stop there. But the verse actually says:

> For the Lord, the God of Israel, saith that he hateth putting away: for one covereth violence with his garment, saith the Lord of Hosts: therefore take heed to your spirit, that ye deal not treacherously.

The phrase "for one covereth violence with his garment" is a very poor translation. The garment is actually speaking of the wife. I think one of the best translations of this verse is found in the Amplified Bible.

> For the Lord, the God of Israel, says: I hate divorce and marital separation, and him who covers his garment [his wife] with violence.

God not only hates divorce, but He hates a man (or woman) who covers his or her mate in violence and then tries to conceal it.

I can't tell you the number of people — usually women — who come into our church for counseling because their spouse is beating them. They are convinced they are "laying down their lives" for their brother and if they continue to love them unconditionally through all the abuse, eventually their mate will repent and turn to the Lord. After all, it is the goodness of God that leads them to repentance, isn't it? And Jesus said we must all take up our cross and follow Him, and He was beaten, too.

This is a satanic perversion of Scripture. A believer may endure physical persecution for the gospel's sake, but God has not ordained marriage or the family to be the place for physical beatings. Marriage was not designed by God as a place of harm. Every Scripture passage we have studied concerning marriage declares it to be a place of love, tenderness and encouragement.

If you are being physically abused by your spouse, especially if you have children, you should separate yourself from the abuser. It is much easier to pray in faith, speak words of faith and walk in forgiveness toward the abusive mate when you are not living with them and with the constant anxiety of them hurting you.

You will only make the situation worse by staying with the abuser. Find a good Christian counselor who can help you (and your children) understand and overcome the cycle of abuse you have entered into in your home.

Your commitment and perseverance to break out of the cycle of abuse may shake up your mate and encourage them to get help. However, in many cases the abuser refuses even to admit they have a problem. Abusers often blame their actions on their spouses and take no responsibility for their violent behavior.

Several conditions must be present before you consider divorce because of physical abuse, however. First, you must have been separated long enough to achieve spiritual, mental and emotional stability apart from the abuser. Second, your husband or wife must have refused to repent or take any steps to change. Third and most important, through prayer, you know that God has released you from and given you peace about dissolving the marriage.

You should never rush into marriage, and you should never rush into divorce, even when you have scriptural grounds.

The second scriptural grounds for divorce is found in 1 Corinthians 7:15-16. The Bible allows a believer to divorce for desertion — one partner leaving the other because he or she is born again.

> But if the unbelieving depart, let him depart. A brother or a sister is not under bondage in such cases: but God hath called us to peace. For what knowest thou, O wife, whether thou shalt save thy husband? or how knowest thou, O man, whether thou shalt save thy wife?

When there are two believers in a marriage, and one deserts the other, the Bible encourages them to do all they can to reconcile and restore their marriage. But if your unbelieving mate walks out and divorces you, you are not obligated by God to pursue them. Don't chase them down the street and promise anything to get them to come back.

The Bible also does not say to believe God and pray they will come back.

First Corinthians 7:15 says God has called us to peace. It is difficult to maintain peace in the home if your spouse does not accept or respect your faith. If the unbeliever is pleased to dwell with the believer, then it is a different matter. But desertion and divorce indicate the unbeliever is not pleased to dwell with the believer.

I've had church members come into my office who have been separated or divorced from an unbelieving mate for a year or more. They ask me, "What should I do?" I show them these Scripture verses and tell them to let their unbelieving husband or wife go. The Word of God says the believer is not responsible for getting the unbelieving mate saved; neither is the believer bound to the unbelieving spouse if he or she departs.

> And when she is departed out of his house, she may go and be another man's wife. And if the latter husband hate her, and write her a bill of divorcement, and giveth it in her hand, and sendeth her out of his house; or if the latter husband die, which took her to be his wife; her former husband, which sent her away, may not take her again to be his wife, after that she is defiled; for that is abomination before the Lord: and thou shalt not cause the land to sin, which the Lord thy God giveth thee for an inheritance (Deuteronomy 24:2-4).

I include these verses to point out a misunderstanding regarding "standing for the return of your mate," which has come up in the past few years. Some believers go so far as to stand in faith for the return of a mate even after the departed husband or wife has married someone else. The Word declares this is an abomination to God, because in

197

order for your mate to return, they would have to divorce the one to whom they are presently married.

If you have been divorced, and the one you are divorced from (whether they are saved or not) has remarried, you are free. Trust the Lord for another mate rather than praying in vain for God to sin and break up another marriage.

The third and most well-known scriptural grounds for divorce is fornication. We find this in Matthew 5:31-32, where Jesus says:

> It hath been said, Whosoever shall put away his wife, let him give her a writing of divorcement: But I say unto you, that whosoever shall put away his wife, saving for the cause of fornication.

Jesus is stating that a legitimate grounds for divorce is fornication, or adultery, and He is referring to Deuteronomy 24:1.

> When a man hath taken a wife, and married her, and it come to pass that she find no favour in his eyes, because he hath found some uncleanness in her: then let him write her a bill of divorcement, and give it in her hand, and send her out of his house.

The word *uncleanness* means the same as fornication. Both words denote sexual immorality. I want to point out again that although these verses describe the *woman* as being unclean, the principle could apply just as well if the *man* was involved in sexual immorality.

Jesus caused quite a stir among the scribes and Pharisees when He said "fornication" instead of "uncleanness." You see, by the time Jesus came on the scene, the scribes and Pharisees had expanded the meaning of uncleanness to mean "the breaking of any jot or tittle of the Law." A Jewish man could divorce his wife if she failed in any area of the law.

For example, the Law stated that if you walked into a dead man's room, you were considered unclean until you went through a purification rite. Therefore, if a man grew tired of his wife — if she burned the biscuits too many times or her fried chicken was never as good as his mom's — then he would say, "Honey, why don't you take some cake and cookies down to Brother So-and-So today. I understand he's not feeling too well."

Of course, he knows Brother So-and-So is dead, so when she walks in the room, she becomes unclean. Then her husband is free to declare her unclean and unfit to be his wife. By the time she is on her way home, he has executed a writ of divorcement and posted it on the front door.

I'm sure you are reading this and thinking it is the most bizarre story you've ever heard. But our society is doing the same thing today. Even Christians take the Word of God and stretch it so far that we have divorce for every reason imaginable.

The most ridiculous reason, but one we hear all the time is, "I just don't love them anymore, and God is a God of love, so it is not His will for me to be married to this person anymore." With the Author of love living in their hearts and any knowledge of God's Word in their heads, it is difficult to understand how believers can use "I just don't love them anymore" as grounds for divorce. Yet it happens every day.

When Jesus narrowly defined uncleanness as fornication, the religious Jews were furious with Him. He was taking away their carte-blanche right to marry and divorce on a whim. In essence He was saying, "Boys, marriage is not to be taken lightly. This is a commitment for life, and only if your wife has committed sexual sin can you even consider divorce."

Again, we can turn to Jesus' own words. He equated divorce due to fornication with hardness of heart *toward God*:

And the Pharisees came to him, and asked him, Is it lawful for a man to put away his wife? tempting him. And he answered and said unto them, What did Moses command you? And they said, Moses suffered to write a bill of divorcement, and to put her away. And Jesus answered and said unto them, For the hardness of your heart he wrote you this precept. But from the beginning of the creation God made them male and female.

For this cause shall a man leave his father and mother, and cleave to his wife; and they twain shall be one flesh: so then they are no more twain, but one flesh. What therefore God hath joined together, let not man put asunder (Mark 10:2-9).

If your mate commits adultery and repents, I believe the law of forgiveness should rule in your life. If they are willing to get the godly counseling they need to find and eliminate the root of their sin, and they have committed themselves to working out your marriage problems, then I do not believe you should divorce.

The first thing many Christians do when their spouse falls into adultery is file for divorce. Without confronting their spouse, having a counseling session with their pastor or even praying seriously, they are ready to give up their marriage. They are acting out of their hurt and anger instead of the principles of God's Word: "What therefore God hath joined together, let not man put asunder."

It is hard to forgive any sin that is committed against us, and some sins are harder to forgive than others. Nevertheless, God commands us to forgive those who trespass against us, and the sins of our mates are no exception. If they repent and recommit their life to the Lord and to us, then the marriage can, after a time of emotional healing and rebuilding trust, become strong.

We have already studied fornication and adultery in chapters 2 and 3 of this book. We have seen the destruction and grief these particular sins can cause. That is why, when a spouse *repeatedly* and *unrepentantly* commits sexual sin, Jesus allows for divorce.

It is not God's will for a spouse and children to be continuously exposed to immorality and disease in their own home. Ultimately the spirit of rebellion and hardness of heart toward God in the unclean mate can overpower them, too. So the Word of God declares that sexual sin is grounds for divorce.

Is There Marriage After Divorce?

After a believer is divorced, what then? If they have received forgiveness from the Lord, allowed the Holy Spirit to change and heal them, and become stable in the things of God, does the Bible say they can marry again?

> And when she is departed out of his house, she may go and be another man's wife (Deuteronomy 24:2).

According to this verse you can be remarried after you are divorced. Remarriage is acceptable under the Old Testament law. Many Christians today teach that once you have divorced, that is it — you can never be married again unless you remarry the one you divorced. Here are the Scripture verses believers cite when telling their divorced friends that it is against the Word of God to remarry.

> And unto the married I command, yet not I, but the Lord, Let not the wife depart from her husband: But and if she depart, let her remain unmarried, or be reconciled to her husband: and let not the husband put away his wife (1 Corinthians 7:10-11).

The phrase "depart from her husband" means to leave, separate from or divorce. The command Paul and the Lord gave was: Do not divorce. The Holy Spirit was saying to the Corinthians — and to us today — that divorce is not the answer to our marital problems. When we divorce, we are just exchanging one set of problems for another.

However, we have seen there are scriptural reasons for divorce, and in verse 11 Paul recognizes those reasons when he says, "But and if she depart." He continues by saying she should either remain unmarried or go back to her husband (the same applies for a man and his wife).

God has no problem with you remarrying the person you divorced, but the major issue here is in the first part of verse 11. This says if you divorce you should remain unmarried. Many ministers and church members have assumed this verse meant if you divorce you can never marry again.

This verse is actually saying you should remain unmarried for a time, but you do not have to remain single forever.

When you get divorced, you need to have time to remain single, to recover and work out the problems you have. You shouldn't jump right into another marriage just after you are divorced because there is much confusion and hurt to work through.

Once you have been fully restored, you can marry again and have less chance of bringing those problems into the new marriage. In 1 Corinthians 7:27-28 Paul addresses divorce and then remarriage.

> Art thou bound unto a wife? seek not to be loosed. Art thou loosed from a wife? seek not a wife. But and if thou marry, thou hast not sinned; and if a virgin marry, she hath not sinned. Nevertheless such shall have trouble in the flesh: but I spare you.

He says that if you are bound (married), do all you can

to avoid being loosed (divorced). If you are loosed (divorced), don't immediately look for another mate. But if you do get married again (v.28), *you have not sinned.* Many Christians could have been saved a lot of sorrow if *all* the verses of 1 Corinthians 7 had been taught.

The next part of verse 28, "and if a virgin marry, she hath not sinned," should be put in parentheses. Why would Paul say this? Everyone knows that if a virgin marries she is not sinning. But that is the point of this verse — a person who has divorced and married again later is no more in sin than a virgin who marries for the first time.

Trouble in the Flesh — But Spared

Paul lets those who have been divorced know they have the freedom to remarry after a reasonable period of time. Still, he goes on to warn them they will have more trouble in a subsequent marriage "in the flesh." This means there are problems that occur in subsequent marriages which are less likely to occur in a first marriage.

Spiritually, you and your spouse are one flesh and know God brought you together. But one or both of you may have to deal with spouses and children from previous marriages. One of the greatest challenges in the Church today is what the world calls stepfamilies. However, I cannot find any Scripture verse in the Bible that refers to a concept such as stepfamilies.

God is in the business of building *families,* and the key issue is *authority.* When a man and a woman marry, they leave the authority of their parents (Genesis 2:24), and this principle applies to remarriage also. When a woman divorces and later remarries, she and any children she brings to the marriage are under the authority of her new husband. Any children her new husband brings to the marriage are subject to her authority as well.

When the children are in your home, they should understand and respect the authority of their new parent. Children may not like their stepparent, or they may be unwilling to accept their new parent's authority, but when their mother and stepfather (or vice versa) said "I do," they spoke for the children, too.

So much depends on how you prepare children for the change. From the moment you are engaged to be married, both of you must be very clear — between yourselves and with the children — about your respective roles regarding them. In that way you will defeat any attempt of the enemy to destroy your new family by using the children to come between you.

You and your mate must stand together in agreement. Be unified against every challenge to the well-being of your new family. These children will not be under your roof for long, but you and your mate will spend the rest of your lives together. Besides, the best thing parents can do for their children is to show them a good marriage.

This next passage of Scripture can help children look beyond the natural situation and understand the spiritual reality of their new family.

> Give ear, O my people, to my law: incline your ears to the words of my mouth. I will open my mouth in a parable: I will utter dark sayings of old: Which we have heard and known, and our fathers have told us (Psalms 78:1-3).

Notice that the word *fathers* is plural. It is no accident that one of the names for the Church, or the Body of Christ, is "the family of God." We are a family. We are all brothers and sisters in Christ, and we can all have many fathers and mothers in the faith.

A child can find comfort in the multipurpose will of God. If their mother or father knows their new spouse is the one God brought to them, the children can also know this is the right parent for them. Children can come to love and appreciate their new parent if they understand from the Word how they are just as much a "father" or "mother" to them as a biological parent.

We can turn the tables on this principle and apply it to the new parent also. If you marry someone with growing children, you may have trouble seeing them as your responsibility. You may also find it difficult to love them — especially if they are hostile toward you. Then you too must look to Psalm 78:3! If God put you and your mate together, He will give you the grace to be a godly parent to those children.

It goes without saying that dealing with ex-spouses should not jeopardize your new family either. Some relationships with former spouses are friendly, but most are not. In any situation, it is best to draw large, clear lines and stick to them. You and your mate, the children and the ex-spouses should understand the guidelines you and your wife or husband have established for your new family.

I realize all this is easier said than done. There are whole books devoted to this subject, and I am just giving a few principles. However, in 1 Corinthians 7:28 Paul goes on to say, "I spare you." Paul wants people spared because no problem is insurmountable through Jesus Christ — even a second, third or fourth marriage. God's grace is always sufficient. The challenge may be great, but the power of God is greater. Joy and happiness can be found no matter what the circumstances.

Parenting With Jesus

Another situation many believers face, which is also growing rapidly in the Church, is single parenthood. Again, the same grace that sees us through every other challenge in our lives can see the single parent through. In fact, there are several Scripture passages which are particularly encouraging to single-parent families.

> For thy Maker is thine husband; the Lord of hosts is his name; and thy Redeemer the Holy One of Israel; the God of the whole earth shall he be called (Isaiah 54:5).

The Lord declares He is the widow's husband (this could refer to the divorced person or the widower). Just as the Lord is the single person's sufficiency in all things, He will be the single parent's sufficiency in all things.

> And all thy children shall be taught of the Lord; and great shall be the peace of thy children (Isaiah 54:13).

Here the Lord assures you He will personally teach your children. This does not mean you are absolved of any responsibility to teach and discipline them. What it means is that when you do, He will stand with you and reveal Himself to them.

God Himself will back you up!

Also, we can look again to Psalm 78:3, which tells us we have many fathers and mothers in the faith. This is one of the functions of the local church: to provide you with the family members who are missing from your natural family. Children of a single parent can find wonderful fathers and mothers in their church — believers who will impart the Word of God to them and help them live it; men and women who will fill the gap their absent father or mother has left.

This principle holds for children with both parents, too. Although I was fortunate to have wonderful, godly parents who never divorced, there have been other "parents" in the Lord who have had a tremendous influence on my life. And sometimes another adult in the Body of Christ can speak things to your child that you cannot.

Parenting is never easy, whether or not you have a spouse to help in this responsibility. But it is always Jesus who makes the difference. With children, you face situations in which only divine revelation will see you through!

> If any of you lack wisdom, let him ask of God, that giveth to all men liberally, and upbraideth not; and it shall be given him (James 1:5).

This is a Scripture verse for raising children! Any believer who is a parent knows there are times when only the Holy Spirit can tell you what to do or say. Only by His wisdom and grace can any of us raise godly children to shine in an ungodly world.

A Grim Reality— But Jesus Can Bring a Happy Ending

As a pastor this is one of the realities I must face: Christians are not perfect, and some do get divorced. They are not immune to the wiles, devices and deceptions of the devil. Dealing with divorce is part of being in the Body of Christ, and we should extend the same grace to the repentant divorced person that we extend to anyone else in the Church who is hurting. Those who are divorced have not committed the unpardonable sin, and in some cases they have not sinned at all.

Some divorced people are innocent, standing by in horror as their world falls apart. They watch their spouse fall and refuse to repent, then exit the marriage with no regrets. When they turn to their church for help, often they are told they must repent of *their* sin of divorce and are treated coldly. Their torn heart is now subjected to condemnation and isolation from other believers.

Others are the cause of their divorce, and it is my job to point out their scriptural error, calling them to repentance and praying they will choose to turn from their sin and be restored to their mate. If they do repent, often their wounded mate refuses to accept them back. Although they have returned to fellowship with the Lord, the wronged spouse divorces them for the sins of the past. In many cases they are viewed as terminally guilty and shunned by other believers.

If you were the cause of your divorce and have not taken responsibility for your sin, I must tell you that peace will never be yours until you surrender yourself to God, repent and dedicate yourself to conforming your life to His Word. But if you fall into one of the two categories of divorced people I just mentioned, I have great news for you.

Like Joseph, you can forgive and place your life into the hands of the Lord, allowing Him to restore you. Whether you are still reeling with anger and hurt or are just trying to understand what happened, He has healing and wisdom for you. Turn from any resentment and self-pity, which can only destroy you, and trust in Him. If you do this, the peace God has promised will flood your daily life.

Divorced people are still people, and God is in the business of doing miracles in people's lives. Just as we expect Him to move miraculously in the lives of those who are in other difficult situations, we should pray and believe for Him to move miraculously in the divorced person's life.

I challenge all believers to help and support those in their churches who have been divorced and desire to be restored, especially the innocent ones (and any children) who are in deep emotional pain. They need your steadfast friendship to get through the transition from being married to being single. And they need prayer partners who will see them not as a divorced person but a child of God. 🕭

NINE

THE HUSBAND'S HEART — HER SIGNATURE

A virtuous woman is a crown to her husband" (Proverbs 12:4). The Bible declares the husband is king of the home, and the wife is his crown, but what does it mean for her to be his crown? The crown is the outward show and validation of his kingship, and it encircles his head, which represents his soul. The virtuous wife has captured the soul of her husband, and in return for his love and adoration, she crowns him with her honor and respect.

No doubt, when Solomon was inspired by the Holy Spirit to write these words, he was thinking about his father and mother, David and Bathsheba. There are many virtuous women in the Bible, but Bathsheba was Solomon's personal example of what a godly woman, wife and mother should be. And David, the man after God's own heart, was the king whom she crowned with honor and respect.

Shaky Beginnings

If there ever was a marriage that should have failed, it was David and Bathsheba's. Yet theirs became one of the Bible's best examples of a one-flesh relationship. Their story, which began with adultery, is well-known even among unbelievers. Although many blame Bathsheba for being promiscuous, she was actually an innocent victim.

> And it came to pass, after the year was expired, at the time when kings go forth to battle...David tarried still at Jerusalem (2 Samuel 11:1).

It was the time when kings go to battle, but King David had chosen to stay at home. While all of his men were on the battlefield fighting, he was taking a little vacation. He was out of God's will, and when you are out of God's will, the flesh easily takes over.

Israel's great king began sleeping late in the morning and staying up late at night, feeling more and more agitated. Night after night on the roof of his palace he would pace restlessly back and forth, gazing out over the city.

On one of those evenings Bathsheba, assuming all the men were at war where they were supposed to be, innocently took a bath on her porch. David saw her and was sexually ignited by her beauty — but he did not put out the fire. Instead, he sent for her, committed adultery with her, and she became pregnant.

When news of Bathsheba's pregnancy reached him, rather than falling to his knees in repentance, David plunged deeper into sin. Thinking he could cover himself, he had her husband — one of his most loyal officers — killed on the front lines of battle. Then he married her. What a rocky way to begin a marriage!

Bathsheba mourned for her dead husband. She loved him because he had been a great man. She would have a struggle to forgive David. Not only had he committed adultery with her and made her pregnant, killed her husband and forced her to marry him, but because of David's sin the child who was born to them did not live.

Grief was piled upon grief at the start of their marriage, and yet David and Bathsheba turned to God and were able to develop a successful relationship. No doubt the turning point was when David repented (2 Samuel 12:13).

Their marriage produced a second child, Solomon, who later became the wisest king of Israel. But, most important, out of their marriage came the Book of Proverbs, which contains some of the greatest wisdom for husbands and wives.

Bathsheba Speaks Her Mind

Throughout the Book of Proverbs, Solomon speaks of the things his father, David, taught him. But in Proverbs 31, he reveals Bathsheba's wise words to him. She called Solomon by the nickname Lemuel, which means "belonging to the Lord." David and Bathsheba had dedicated Solomon to the Lord at a very young age, and God revealed to them that he would be the next king of Israel.

> The words of king Lemuel, the prophecy that his mother taught him. What, my son? and what, the son of my womb? and what, the son of my vows? (Proverbs 31:1-2).

At the time Bathsheba taught these verses to Solomon, David was dying, and one of his other sons, Adonijah, was setting himself up as king. By referring to Solomon as "the son of my vows," she was confirming again the prophecy that he would succeed his father as king.

Not only did Bathsheba remind her son of his rightful position as heir to the throne, but she also took measures to ensure Solomon's succession. The following passage of Scripture shows how she approached David in this matter.

> And Bathsheba bowed, and did obeisance unto the king. And the king said, What wouldest thou? And she said unto him, My lord, thou swarest by the Lord thy God unto thine handmaid, saying, Assuredly Solomon thy son shall reign after me, and he shall sit upon my throne (1 Kings 1:16-17).

After all David had put her through, she called him lord. Her attitude had changed toward him. Now there was no trace of bitterness or hatred for him, but only love and respect. This illustrates to us that no matter what kind of trouble we are having in our marriage, God can heal it! David's response to her plea comes in verses 28-30:

> Then king David answered and said, Call me Bathsheba. And she came into the king's presence, and stood before the king. And the king sware, and said, As the Lord liveth, that hath redeemed my soul out of all distress, even as I sware unto thee by the Lord God of Israel, saying, Assuredly Solomon thy son shall reign after me, and he shall sit upon my throne in my stead; even so will I certainly do this day.

After Bathsheba humbly reminded David that it was God's will for Solomon to be king, David made an oath:

Solomon would succeed him. Notice how Bathsheba responded to the love and faithfulness of her husband:

> Then Bathsheba bowed with her face to the earth, and did reverence to the king, and said, Let my lord king David live forever (1 Kings 1:31).

The relationship we see here is a wife who crowns her husband with honor in response to his affection and integrity toward her. She is totally submitted to him, and he has proven himself her protector and provider, even in his death.

When David died, Solomon became king as his father had sworn. He was only a teenager, and his mother was his first adviser. Bathsheba proceeded to give the newly crowned, immature king some timely advice in Proverbs 31, but you can be sure that young Lemuel's mind was not on his mother's instructions!

He was more interested in driving his new chariot than learning to be a good king. In verse 2 Bathsheba had to repeat three times, "What, my son?" She was trying to get his undivided attention! The verses that follow tell us why she was so concerned. It seems Solomon was exhibiting two weaknesses very early: He was girl crazy, and he liked to experiment with wine and strong drink.

> Give not thy strength unto women, nor thy ways to that which destroyeth kings. It is not for kings, O Lemuel, it is not for kings to drink wine; nor for princes strong drink: Lest they drink, and forget the law, and pervert the judgment of any of the afflicted (Proverbs 31:3-5).

Apparently Solomon decided to heed his mother's warning about strong drink. The Bible does not record any problems he had in that area, and we know his judgement over the disputes of the people was filled with divine wisdom. It was in the area of women and marriage that he did not follow his parents' advice.

During his reign, Solomon had a physical crown on his head, but he never had a crown over his soul.

Solomon married so many women that he never found that special one who would capture his thoughts and win his heart, crowning him with her honor and respect. Nevertheless he managed to record in Proverbs 31 the beautiful picture of a one-flesh relationship which Bathsheba painted for him.

What Is an Acrostic?

Bathsheba did her best to set her son on the right path in marriage by giving him an acrostic on the subject. Evidently, she learned the art from David, who was the first to write an acrostic in the Word of God.

In an acrostic, each verse begins with a Hebrew letter, following in Hebrew alphabetical order. There are twenty-two letters in the Hebrew alphabet, and every one of the twenty-two verses in Proverbs 31:10-31 begins with a Hebrew letter. For example, verse 10 begins with *aleph*, verse 11 with *beth*, verse 12 with *giymel* and so on.

Furthermore, each one of the Hebrew letters is a depiction of its meaning, adding greater depth to our understanding of the verse. Psalms 25, 37 and 119 are all acrostics, as well as the entire Book of Lamentations.

I believe Bathsheba chose the format of an acrostic because of Solomon's age. Being the curious, scatter-brained teenager he was, having to call him three times before he even looked at her, she probably said, "OK, Lemuel, I'm going to give you the ABCs of marriage. This way you'll be able to remember what I tell you."

Bathsheba is making the Word of God simple for her son — simple to remember and simple to understand.

The Proverbs 31 acrostic begins and ends with the man, while the virtuous woman is spoken of in between. This is symbolic of how a wife's life begins and ends with her husband, just as the Church's life begins and ends with the Lord Jesus Christ.

> Husbands, love your wives, even as Christ also loved the church, and gave himself for it; that he might sanctify and cleanse it with the washing of water by the word, that he might present it to himself a glorious church, not having spot, or wrinkle, or any such thing; but that it should be holy and without blemish (Ephesians 5:25-27).

Notice that verse 25 is past tense, verse 26 is present tense and verse 27 is future tense. The Church began after Jesus, the aggressor and initiator, gave Himself for her and was resurrected. Now He is continuously maturing her and cleansing her as she responds to His Word. In the future He will present her to Himself in perfection, the Bride of Christ.

Bathsheba's acrostic in Proverbs 31 is laid out in the same manner, with the husband in the beginning and final verses and the wife in the middle.[1]

Bathsheba's Acrostic to Lemuel

 Who can find a virtuous woman? for her price is far above rubies (Proverbs 31:10).

The first Hebrew letter of this verse is *aleph*, which is the symbol of *prosperity*.

Aleph, which indicated great riches, is a picture of two oxen yoked together. If you owned oxen in the ancient world, you were extremely wealthy. The virtuous woman is first compared to oxen because she is her husband's most valuable gift from God.

Throughout this acrostic you will find some strange comparisons, and many of them may even sound insulting by today's standards and thinking. However, if we see these things through the eyes of the ancient people, we can understand the full significance of their symbolism.

For instance, we have already seen how the "roe" in Proverbs 5:19 represents a she-goat. Today our response would be, "See, honey, I told you it was scriptural to call you an old goat!"

However, in the ancient world, one of the most powerful symbols of symmetry, grace and beauty was the she-goat. It was a high compliment for a woman to be likened to one.

The oxen represented tremendous prosperity, and only the very wealthy offered oxen as sacrifices to the Lord. The virtuous woman is likened to a team of oxen because she is the most important person in her husband's life other than God. His relationship with her is a key to his success in every area of his life. Her value is far above rubies!

The following verses amplify verse 10, giving us more detail on how a wife is the most prized gift God gives a man.

 The heart of her husband doth safely trust in her, so that he shall have no need of spoil (Proverbs 31:11).

This verse begins with the Hebrew letter *beth*, which is the picture of a house with only one door. This speaks of total *trust*.

When a husband is able to share his whole life with his wife and know his confidences are safe with her, his heart trusts in her. The security he enjoys at home is so strong that he feels no need to go after other women (the word *spoil* is symbolic of adultery). Why should a husband go out and steal a used car when he's got a luxury model at home?

A marriage is not based on the goose bumps of love but on the trust of friendship. Romance is good, but it is the time you devote to developing friendship and trust with your mate that will keep your marriage together.

The letter *beth* indicates the house is not merely a building where a family lives, but a home. A home is a place of love, fellowship and communication — a place where you like to spend your time. For this husband and wife, their home is their favorite place!

 She will do him good and not evil all the days of her life (Proverbs 31:12).

The Hebrew letter *giymel* begins this verse. *Giymel* depicts a camel, and the significant part is its head. The camel's head never moves while it is running, which speaks of *dependability.*

The camel was the most dependable animal in the ancient world. Whether you were going through a forest or over a desert, his head was always up and pointed straight ahead. He kept on going, rain or shine.

The virtuous woman can be depended on by her husband. She is not moved by circumstances; she is only moved by the Word of God. She brings nothing but good to him every day of his life, which means she knows how to endure and persevere. She's not dependable one moment and irresponsible the next, but consistently faithful.

She seeketh wool, and flax, and worketh willingly with her hands (Proverbs 31:13).

Verse 13 begins with *daleth.* This Hebrew letter depicts

an open door as you are looking down upon it. *Daleth* represents *making decisions*.

When Jesus enters our hearts and shows us unconditional love and acceptance, we become secure in who we are. As a result, we become confident in fulfilling His purpose for our lives. Decisions are much easier to make when we know what we are supposed to do — and when we know God Himself is backing us up!

When a husband loves his wife as Jesus loves the Church, she becomes bold and confident in all her activities and responsibilities. She responds to his love by aggressively making decisions in her areas of authority, knowing he trusts her judgment and is behind her all the way.

She doesn't need to ask him about every move she makes. She seeks wool and flax, which represent the clothes she wears when she goes out into the world. Wool is a heavy fabric worn in cold weather; flax is lightweight, something you would wear in the summer. So she dresses sensibly, according to the seasons. Because she is secure, her decisions reflect common sense.

The last part of this verse is wonderful in the Hebrew. It literally says that her hands delight in her work. Now we all know housework is not the greatest pleasure in life, so how could she delight in it? She takes delight in her work because she is doing it for her husband and family, who delight and trust in her.

The same principle holds true for the husband. No matter what mundane tasks he has to do on the job, he can take delight in them, knowing he is providing for her by doing them. Not only do believers do all things as unto the Lord, but husbands and wives carry out their work for each other as well.

This is one of the most important decisions a married person will make: No matter what the day demands, do it gratefully as unto the Lord and for the benefit of your spouse. Delight and trust in each other, and what was drudgery becomes delightful!

**She is like the merchants' ships;
she bringeth her food from afar
(Proverbs 31:14).**

He is the first Hebrew letter of this verse, and it is the picture of a window. He represents *perspective*.

There are three Hebrew letters which symbolize a house: *beth, cheth* and *he*. Each one signifies a different part of the house. *Beth* is the door, *cheth* is the outside walls enclosing the house, and *he* is the window.

The merchant ships of Solomon's day were very famous. They traveled all around the world collecting the finest articles and goods for Solomon's use and display.

With this in mind, the wife does not consider distance a factor when purchasing the things her family needs. She seeks out the best for them. Her perspective is that God has given her a wonderful husband and family, and she wants the best for them.

This does not mean she spends exorbitant amounts of money. She finds the best quality for the price she can afford, even if she has to go across town instead of running to the store around the corner. She has a healthy, balanced perspective in caring for her husband and children.

**She riseth also while it is yet
night, and giveth meat to her
household, and a portion to her
maidens (Proverbs 31:15).**

Vau, or *vav*, the next letter of the Hebrew alphabet, is found at the beginning of this verse. *Vau* is the picture of a hook or peg, such as a hook on which you might hang your coat when you come home. In other words, the whole family hangs upon the virtuous woman; *they rest upon her.*

This verse speaks of how the wife is the foundation of her home. The saying is true that "a man works from sun to sun, but a woman's work is never done." Bathsheba wanted Solomon to understand the many different tasks a wife has. Often a husband doesn't see anything but a clean house; food on the table; healthy, happy children; and ironed shirts in his closet. He doesn't know the time, effort and planning it takes for his wife to do these things on a daily basis.

Proverbs 31:15 says the virtuous woman gets up early to prepare the food for her family, and we know from the previous verse that she has taken great care in choosing the food. But, wives, it also says she assigns tasks to her maids! According to the Bible, there is nothing wrong with hiring help to do the housework if you can afford it.

I also want you to notice she didn't get up early just to set out a menu. She decided what the family would be eating for the day. It is up to the wife to set good nutritional habits in the home. If she leaves it to her family, they will be eating junk food!

 She considereth a field, and buyeth it: with the fruit of her hands she planteth a vineyard (Proverbs 31:16).

The Hebrew letter *zayin,* which is the shape of a sword, begins verse 16. *Zayin* represents the virtuous woman's *zeal and tenacity.*

When she considers a business transaction — once she has peace from God and confirmation from her husband — she seizes the opportunity and takes full advantage of it. Not only does she purchase the field, but she immediately begins to cultivate it.

She is never satisfied with the status quo, but is continuously looking for more God-given opportunities to improve her family's way of life and standard of living. She taps into

God's grace more and more. She pulls out her sword (the Word) and goes after the high ground (prosperity). Once she takes it, she doesn't let it go.

She knows it is God's will for her family to succeed, and therefore she takes advantage of every door He opens to her. But she guards against becoming so involved in her business that her family suffers. Instead, her zeal and tenacity in business transactions is to bless them.

 She girdeth her loins with strength, and strengtheneth her arms (Proverbs 31:17).

Cheth is the next Hebrew letter and the third one that represents a house. *Cheth* is the symbol for an *enclosure*.

A wife is the physical enclosure for her husband. No matter how tired she is, when he comes home she draws upon her inner strength to meet him and surround him with her love. Her sexual passion for him puts a supernatural hedge of protection around his life.

Bathsheba also used the word *strength* in verse 3. She instructed Solomon not to give his sexual strength to women but to save himself for his wife. Now Bathsheba lets a wife know she should take the time to refresh herself and have an attitude to please her husband sexually.

"Stengtheneth her arms" actually means that she encourages her arms to meet him. She throws her arms around him as though she had done nothing but think about him all day.

If you consider all this woman has done in the last four verses, this is amazing. She bought material for clothing and made the clothes; she traveled far, if necessary, to get the best buy on the best food; she awoke early to prepare the food and delegate household chores to her staff; and she purchased a field and planted a vineyard.

I'm sure she did some of these things every day and others over a period of days. Still, after all this activity, you'd think she would be a wreck, and when her husband came home she would say, "Honey, I'm beat. You're on your own tonight." Instead, she chooses to please him.

Husbands, this principle applies to you as well. There are many days when all you want to do is go home, eat and crawl into bed. Nevertheless, you should draw upon your inward strength and show your wife and children the love they deserve.

God does not want a husband coming through the door saying, "What a day. Just feed me and leave me alone." Nor does he want a wife to say, "Well, don't expect me to do anything, because I've had an exhausting day, too." Instead, He gives them the strength to embrace each other.

God grants a supernatural strength for husbands and wives to love one another, and this special grace is not just for times of crisis or disagreement. God's strength is also available for times when you are simply tired but your mate needs you to express your love anyway.

Keeping sexual passion alive builds a solid enclosure of protection around your marriage.

 She perceiveth that her merchandise is good: her candle goeth not out by night (Proverbs 31:18).

Teyth is the Hebrew letter beginning this verse. *Teyth* is a symbol for flow, and the flow this verse refers to comes from the virtuous woman's *spirit*.

Proverbs 20:27 says, "The spirit of man is the candle of the Lord." The candle is actually an oil lamp, and oil is a type of the Holy Spirit in both the Old and New Testaments. So the candle in this verse is speaking of the virtuous woman's spirit.

Her spirit does not go out, even late at night, but it burns bright at all times. The strength she exhibits (v. 17) and the perfection she brings forth in all she does (v. 18) are outward manifestations of her spiritual strength and maturity.

She has established her priorities. The Word of God is most important, and every day she makes time to study, meditate and pray. Then, whatever happens during the rest of the day, the flow of divine wisdom and strength is never cut off.

Even if there is a drought in the land, their harvest will continue to come in, because she is led by her spirit. She can find the best for her family, because her heart and mind are set on the Lord.

She layeth her hands to the spindle, and her hands hold the distaff (Proverbs 31:19).

Yowd, the first letter of verse 19, is the "jot" Jesus referred to when He said He had come to fulfill "every jot and tittle" of the law. It is the smallest mark in the Hebrew alphabet, and it looks like a clenched fist or a hand that is closed. This speaks of the woman's *strength in work.*

Her hands are clenched in work for her family. She makes yarn at the spinning wheel in order to weave clothes for them. No matter how tedious or mundane her task, the light of her spirit does not go out because she is filled with love for the Lord and her family.

Literally, the wife's clenched fist says, "The joy of the Lord is my strength" (Nehemiah 8:10).

She stretcheth out her hand to the poor; yea, she reacheth forth her hands to the needy (Proverbs 31:20).

The Hebrew letter *kaph* begins this verse. *Kaph* is the picture of an outstretched hand, and it indicates *giving.*

It is from the hollow of her hand that the virtuous woman gives to the poor and needy. It is important to note, however, that before she gives to others she first supplies for her own household. Verse 19 comes before verse 20!

So many Christians, when they first learn the scriptural principles of giving, give away so much that their families suffer. But the Word of God always says to provide for your own first. When your priorities are in order, you will always have plenty left over for those who are less fortunate.

This verse raises an important point. The wife and mother is in full-time ministry like no one else. She ministers in the home as well as everywhere else she goes during her days. She ministers to her children, to her friends — even to the plumber who has come to fix the plumbing. Remember, you do not have to be a pulpit minister to pray for people, lead them to Jesus or give them food and clothing.

Wives, if you are called into a ministry, always remember that your home comes first. God can get any believer to go on the road and minister to others, but your husband has only *you* for his wife, and your children have only *you* for their mother. God will never call a man or woman into ministry in sacrifice of their home.

The outstretched hand of the virtuous woman is generous and kind, but she will have already met the needs of the family before she reaches out to others.

 She is not afraid of the snow for her household: for all her household are clothed with scarlet (Proverbs 31:21).

This verse begins with the Hebrew letter *lamed*, which looks like an ox goad. Lamed is what Jesus was referring to when He said to Saul, blinded on the road to Damascus, "It is hard for thee to kick against the pricks" (Acts 9:5). The Greek word for "pricks" means an ox goad. This is a *motivator!*

When an ox was frightened or faced an obstacle in its path, it would stop and not move. So the farmer had to prod the animal with an ox goad until it started to move again. We are talking about a powerful motivator!

The virtuous woman is motivated by the Word of God in her heart, which prods her to prepare and keep herself strong in faith for whatever lies ahead. As a result, she is prepared for any crisis or obstacle the devil brings to her door. She knows God's Word will prevail, and she is not afraid.

The color scarlet is a type of royalty. It is a crimson red, like the blood Jesus shed on Calvary. Jesus' blood cleanses us from sin spiritually and heals us of sickness and disease physically. So the clothing the virtuous woman makes for her family is double-layered. One layer symbolizes right standing with God, and the other obedience to prepare in the natural. Her family's scarlet, double-layered clothing represents both natural and supernatural protection.

When anything tries to intimidate or hinder the virtuous woman, God's truth inside of her is the goad that dispels all fear and urges her to press on in adversity. Because she has built herself up spiritually and met her responsibilities in the natural, nothing can cause her to lose faith.

 She maketh herself coverings of tapestry; her clothing is silk and purple (Proverbs 31:22).

Mem, which is the picture for water, is the Hebrew letter that begins verse 22. In Scripture a well of water represents the wife, and a fountain of water represents the husband. In the context of marriage, water represents sexuality.

The coverings of tapestry the virtuous woman makes are bed coverings, and she is dressed in the finest clothing for one very important reason: She has planned a night of pleasure with her husband.

The "finest clothing" for this occasion is sexy lingerie, not old flannel pajamas! Revealing and alluring clothing worn by a married woman in her bedroom is not evil. The world has taken something good and used it for immoral purposes.

Part of the routine of married life should be special evenings for just the two of you. You can expand this to include vacations for just the two of you. My wife and I regularly take off for a few days without the children to spend time together, away from our responsibilities at work and at home.

We saw in the Book of Genesis that God created marriage for pleasure and fulfillment, but so often the pressures of daily living cause sex to become a routine duty and obligation. Husbands and wives need times to play together! Renewing love and friendship brings waters of refreshing to daily married life.

 Her husband is known in the gates, when he sitteth among the elders of the land (Proverbs 31:23).

Verse 23 begins with the letter *nuwn*. *Nuwn* is the Hebrew letter for a fish, which in ancient times symbolized *concentration*.

A husband can concentrate fully on his work when he knows all is well at home. There is no way a man can perform his best on the job if things are not right in his marriage.

The worst time of my ministry was when my wife and I were having problems. I would get up to preach, and the words I had studied so diligently would come out of my mouth, but they had no impact. It was only when we got rid of the strife in our home that the Holy Spirit could move through me as I ministered.

There have been and are ministers whose wives are in sin or are completely opposed to their faith (John Wesley was one such minister). Although this is a difficult and often painful situation, with strong elders in the Lord supporting them in prayer and counsel, they can fulfill the ministry to which they are called. In these cases God gives special grace.

But some ministers are either in sin or refuse to meet their responsibilities to their families. They justify their negligence and sin because they are anointed in the pulpit.

Because "the gifts and calling of God are without repentance" (Romans 11:29), a minister or a professional can be successful while in sin or while ignoring the needs of his wife and family — to a point. But he will never reach his full potential in God (see 1 Peter 3:7).

The hardest thing for me to admit was that I needed Loretta. A man likes to believe he can do everything on his own, that he doesn't need a good relationship with his wife to fulfill his calling or profession. This is nothing more than pride. To have an intimate relationship with God and a successful ministry, I needed to have an intimate, successful relationship with Loretta.

The husband in this verse is someone who bears great responsibilities. The word *gates* refers to governments and indicates this man is in a position of great authority in the country. Bathsheba was probably thinking of David, who was king of Israel, and the burdens she had helped him shoulder throughout the years. Her excellence in the home allowed him to concentrate on affairs of state.

The next verses sound as if they are about the woman, but actually they are an extension, or rather a *reflection*, of this verse about the man. They tell specifically how the husband draws strength from his wife, how she stands with him in all he does, and the honor she brings him.

 She maketh fine linen, and selleth it; and delivereth girdles unto the merchant (Proverbs 31:24).

Camek, the Hebrew letter which begins this verse, is a fulcrum or a support point which keeps everything in balance. Here we are talking about financial stability.

Specifically, *camek* depicts *financial balance.*

I believe that when the children are growing up, it is God's will for the husband to provide all the finances so the wife can be home with the children. For this reason, I encourage couples who are just starting out to wait to have children until their finances are reasonably stable.

Living in a fallen world, few people ever come to a place of continuous financial stability. There are going to be ups and downs and many challenges. In a marriage, the wife can be the balancing point.

When there is not enough income to support the family, she can seek employment for a season to make up the difference. When this happens, the husband must take a greater share of the responsibilities at home and with the children.

A wife can also work outside the home because God has called her to a profession or ministry. The Bible is not against a wife having a career or ministry as long as her husband and family come first. For example, she should try to schedule her day so she can be home when her children are at home, even through the teenage years.

Women in both the Old and New Testaments had specific jobs. Ruth and Naomi, both widows, worked in the fields to support themselves. The first person Paul led to Christ in Philippi was a woman named Lydia, who was a traveling seller of purple — and Paul didn't command her to stay at home after she received the Lord.

That the virtuous woman made and sold these particular items is not the issue. The issue is to maintain financial balance without sacrificing the family. The husband is not the only one who needs to be careful to put his family before his profession or ministry.

 Strength and honour are her clothing; and she shall rejoice in time to come (Proverbs 31:25).

Ayin, the first Hebrew letter of verse 25, is the picture of a fountain. This is not to be confused with the symbol of a fountain as a type of the man's sexual strength. This fountain represents *honor*.

A fountain requires tremendous pressure underneath to push up the water. This point of tremendous energy is the place from which the virtuous woman draws her strength from God. It is the place from which she chooses to do right; it is therefore the origin of honor.

When a woman draws her strength from within, focusing more on the development of her heart than the adorning of her body, strength and honor clothe her. We studied this in 1 Peter 3:3-4, where Peter exhorts women to adorn the "hidden man of the heart." He says that by keeping her priorities in line with Scripture, a wife becomes a precious ornament to the Lord and to her husband.

When a wife's priorities are out of line, she can cause embarrassment and even dishonor to her husband. If she gives in to restlessness and distraction, is constantly on the run, often getting involved in worthy causes to justify her flight, or is consumed with television programs, she will fall. Keeping priorities in line avoids dishonor.

This verse in Proverbs 31 also says she will "rejoice in time to come." In other words, as she grows older, she will just laugh. In a world where getting old is one of the greatest fears we have, the woman who laughs at her wrinkles is a rare find!

The harvest she reaps from her honorable way of life is that the storms of life do not age her or beat her down as the years go by. Instead, her strength and wisdom increase, making her even more beautiful.

From the fountain of wisdom within, the virtuous woman brings honor to her husband.

She openeth her mouth with wisdom; and in her tongue is the law of kindness (Proverbs 31:26).

Phe, or *Pe,* is the Hebrew letter which begins verse 26. This letter depicts an open mouth with a tongue in the middle of it. This verse is speaking of *the social relationship between a husband and wife.*

Because the virtuous woman is clothed with strength and honor, when she opens her mouth to speak, she doesn't detract from the conversation or speak foolishly. She adds wisdom — but with love, not haughtiness. Her tongue has the law of kindness in it. Therefore her husband is never worried about what she might say or whether or not she will embarrass him.

Nothing is worse than being at a party with people who love to talk about things of which they know nothing. Trying to impress people, they make complete fools of themselves because they lack wisdom. Then there are those who use the Word of God as a sword to run others through. They have great "head" knowledge of the Word, but they have not mixed it with love in their hearts. They lack kindness and consideration for others.

Imagine what it would be like to be married to one of these people. Whether they lack wisdom or kindness or both, it is embarrassing to everyone when they open their mouths to speak, but it is especially embarrassing to their spouse. There is an old saying, "You can dress her up but you can't take her out." How sad to be married to a woman who looks great, but every time she opens her mouth, you want to crawl into a hole.

One of the biggest benefits of being married to a virtuous woman or to a godly man is being able to socialize with them without fear of being embarrassed or criticized. You are uplifted and enriched by their conversation, and they are a joy for you to be with, either alone or with others.

She looketh well to the ways of her household, and eateth not the bread of idleness (Proverbs 31:27).

This verse begins with *tsadey,* the Hebrew letter that depicts a reaping hook. Verse 27 tells us that after the virtuous woman has been faithful to sow in all areas mentioned in the previous verses, she will reap her *spiritual harvest.*

It begins by saying, "She looketh well to the ways of her household," but literally this means, "She is spiritually alert to what is going on in her home."

Sometimes everything looks right in the natural, but my wife knows in her spirit that something is wrong in the home — whether it is with me, our children or something else. She is spiritually alert because she has not been idle regarding the Word of God. She has been faithful to study and pray, and this has made her spiritually sensitive.

When a wife's priorities are right and her time with the Lord comes before everything else, her husband and children are blessed in all areas of their lives. Then she knows how to pray for them, how to advise them and what to do for them.

This verse introduces the harvest of blessings she receives, as noted in the final verses.

 Her children arise up, and call her blessed; her husband also, and he praiseth her (Proverbs 31:28).

Verse 28 begins with the Hebrew letter *qowph,* which represents the back of the head. As she patiently sows good seed into her husband's and children's lives, the virtuous woman may not always hear their gratitude and praise for her efforts. But they will praise her *behind her back.*

Her children will call her blessed when they "arise up."

231

This does not mean her young children get up in the morning and greet her with, "Mom, you're the greatest blessing of my life." Most likely she will hear, "Mom, I'm hungry. Can we have pancakes instead of cereal today?"

The phrase "arise up" actually means to grow up. It is only after the children grow up and have to do things for themselves that they begin to realize and appreciate all their mother has done for them through the years. When that happens, it is a great harvest for her. Until that time, however, she may not hear a lot of praise and thanks from them.

She may not hear a lot of praise and thanks from her husband either. Many a man can only praise his wife to someone else. He has a difficult time praising her directly to her face. But this verse is saying she can be sure he is praising her behind her back.

 Many daughters have done virtuously, but thou excellest them all (Proverbs 31:29).

Reysh, which begins this verse, is the Hebrew letter symbolizing the front of the head. This verse is bringing the husband's praise *directly to his wife's face.*

This husband spoke these words directly to his wife. Husband, you need to tell your wife — not just once, but all the time — that she is the best thing that ever happened to you. If she's feeling down, don't buy her a new blender. Tell her what she means to you — to her face (then buy her the blender)!

Beyond just complimenting her, this husband is telling her that no one is better than she. He is so in love with her that there is no doubt in his mind that she is the perfect woman for him.

We all have a tendency to wonder whether there is just one person on this earth meant for us, and whether or not the one we are married to is that person. My wife and I have talked about this. I have wondered if she would have been happier with someone else, and she's wondered if I would have been happier with someone else. We found our answer in this verse.

The Holy Spirit is saying that there are many out there with whom you could be happy, but there is one special person who will make you happier than any other — your spouse. There are many virtuous women in the world, but none of them could make me happy the way Loretta does. To me, she excels them all.

 Favour is deceitful, and beauty is vain: but a woman that feareth the Lord, she shall be praised (Proverbs 31:30).

Siyn, or *shiyn,* begins verse 30. This Hebrew letter looks like a big chewing tooth, and it symbolizes *meditation.*

What is it that the virtuous woman "chews on" all day? What dominates her thoughts? The Word of God! My personal translation of this verse would be, "Elegance is a lie, and dazzling looks are empty, but a woman who meditates on Scripture is a knockout!"

When a woman loves and reverences God above all else, when she seeks the kingdom of God first, not only will her husband and family love and appreciate her, but she will also earn the respect and admiration of the public.

What happens when a wife spends her days and nights meditating in God's Word? This woman is not consumed with who is sleeping with whom on the daily soap operas, all the mundane issues of talk shows, or fantasizing about what might have been. Consequently, her inner beauty transforms her outer beauty into someone people instinctively admire and praise.

Give her of the fruit of her hands; and let her own works praise her in the gates (Proverbs 31:31).

The last verse of the acrostic begins with *thav*, or *tav*. This Hebrew letter is the emblem of a *signature*.

When you come to the end of a letter, what do you do? You sign it. This verse is Bathsheba's — or the virtuous woman's — signature. In marriage, the wife's signature is written on her husband's heart. This verse tells us what is written on the heart of her husband. As he looks at his life and the world around him, how has she made a difference?

"The fruit of her hands" is the harvest she reaps from all she has done for him in their home. In Bathsheba's case, God honored her faithfulness so much that praise of her reached the highest authorities and governments (the gates). Even the officials of King David's government recognized the blessing she brought to David's life and reign.

The fruit of her hands is seen in her husband's success in business and his exemplary reputation in the community, possibly even in the nation. But her works are also shown by her children and how they have grown up to become godly, productive and happy citizens.

Whenever I hear a Christian passionately defend a doctrinal belief, I say, "Let me see the fruit of what you believe." Jesus didn't say you would know people by their beliefs or their teaching — but by their fruit. When we truly live what we believe, there is no need to argue our point. All we have to do is point to the fruit!

Supernatural Marriage

When I taught the Proverbs 31 acrostic of the virtuous woman at our church, many of the women came up to me or wrote me notes saying, "How can I possibly attain to such high standards as these? There is no way I can do all this — I'm not Superwoman, you know!"

My reply was, "You are Superwoman! You may not do the exact same things as the woman Bathsheba describes, but your attitude and life goals can be the same."

And the wives are not the only ones on whom the Bible places superhuman demands. Husbands are to love their wives as Jesus loves the Church. That is a tall order for any man. "What do you mean, be like Jesus? No one can be like Jesus!" But God has given all believers the grace and supernatural strength to attain every goal He has given.

The one-flesh relationship described in Proverbs 31 is not a far-fetched ideal which worked for David and Bathsheba in a much simpler era but is unrealistic for us. This is a way of life God offers to all couples in every generation. His principles for marriage are true for all situations and circumstances.

> For ye are yet carnal: for whereas there is among you envying, and strife, and divisions, are ye not carnal, and walk as men? (1 Corinthians 3:3).

The Amplified Bible translates the last part of this verse,

> Are you not unspiritual and of the flesh, behaving yourselves after a human standard and like mere (unchanged) men?

We are not called to walk as "mere" men, because we are children of the Most High!

If we find our marriage is in trouble with envying, strife and division, we had better ask ourselves if we've been living as "mere" men. Have we been following our own self-centered desires instead of loving and honoring our spouse as the gift of grace they are? Have we fallen into unforgiveness, laziness or pride? Have we neglected to appropriate supernatural wisdom from the Word and supernatural strength from the Holy Spirit?

Your marriage should reflect the wisdom, the blessing, the honor and the glory of the One you follow. Open your spiritual eyes and look past the facade of the natural. See the big "S" on your chest! God put it there when you became His child. Through Jesus Christ you are superman and superwoman, established on God's promises and empowered by His Holy Spirit.

Something wonderful happens when you draw upon His Spirit to line your marriage up with His truth. When a husband loves his wife as Jesus loves the Church, and his wife responds in passionate submission, the whole world sees how marriage for believers is supernatural. The wife's signature is written upon her husband's heart by nothing less than the grace and miraculous power of God.

When a husband and wife set their hearts and minds on eternal things, their harvest is eternal. All the years of putting God first, living uncompromised lives according to His Word, following the guidance of the Holy Spirit and imparting these things to their children reap the blessings of God for many generations.

There is no greater witness of God's unconditional, awesome love than a husband and wife who are *One Flesh*. 🕊

NOTES

Chapter 1

1. *Gleanings in Genesis* (Chicago, Ill.: Moody Press, 1979), p. 11; Jamieson, Fausset and Brown, *Critical and Explanatory Commentary on the Whole Bible,* (Grand Rapids, Mich.: Zondervan Publishing House, n.d.), p. 1; Finis Jennings Dake, *Dake's Annotated Reference Bible,* (Lawrenceville, Ga.: Dake's Bible Sales Inc., 1991), pp. 51-52.

Chapter 9

1. Some acrostic information and definitions were taken from William Gesenius's *Hebrew and Chaldee Lexicon of the Old Testament,* Grand Rapids, Mich.: Baker Book House/Revell, 1984.

Other books by Bob Yandian, available from
Bob Yandian Ministries
P.O. Box 55236
Tulsa, OK 74155
(918) 252-1611
www.precepts.com

God's Word to Pastors
Understanding and Strengthening the Relationship
Between the Pastor and His Congregation

Calling and Separation
Opening the Door to Your Ministry

One Nation Under God
The Rise or Fall of a Nation

Oil and Wine
The Indwelling and Infilling of the Holy Spirit

Salt and Light
The Sermon on the Mount

Decently and in Order
A Guide to New Testament Church Government

Resurrection
Our Victory Over Death

Ephesians
The Maturing of the Saints

Proverbs
Principles of Wisdom

Galatians
The Spirit-Controlled Life

Joel
The Outpouring of God's Glory